Riding My Dreams

My Stories From A Boy To A Man

Bruce Sparks

To my FRIEND BRENDA
Love Always
Bruce Sparks

Riding My Dreams

Granite Publishing

1551055906

Prescott Dover Dublin

ISBN 978-1-950105-53-3

Riding My Dreams

Dedication

Georgia Sparks (1954 - 2020)

The two most important dates in my life are the day I was born
and the day I found out why.
That day was the day I met Georgia.
I promised her I would get this book printed.
This book is dedicated to her.

Preface

These are the true stories, memories, and reflections of a boy growing up in a small farming town in Southwest Arizona. It is about how the author, as a young boy, found life and how to deal with it through his love for horses. It's about a place of heat and relentless sunshine, where shade and water were the best things one could find. Yuma was the town and is the place where restaurants will give you a free meal any day the Sun doesn't shine. It's the story of how a boy grew into a man's world quickly.

Horses, as this boy came to know them, were born and bred for sport, and his calling as a Bronc Rider was heard early in his youth. Not growing up on a farm or around livestock didn't diminish the drive this boy found in rodeo sports and in particular Saddle Bronc Riding.

From grade school throughout his high school years, the adventures he shared with his brother are the stories to be told in his time with horses. The ups and downs, the happiness and the pain were what led this boy to seek out his own worth in a man's world. These are those stories.

Acknowledgments

It should be noted that the cover design stems from a photograph taken of the author well over a half-century ago. The process of viewing the photograph and creating a fine piece of art goes to the credit of artist Mary Dove. Prints of the author, Bruce Sparks, riding this bucking bronc in a long-forgotten Arizona Rodeo are readily available and can be easily viewed online. The image used for the cover was, digitally altered, touched up, and enhanced by digital artist Susan Grant.

It should also be acknowledged that the editor faced the enormous challenge of trying to keep the Southwest local dialogue and idiosyncratic form of writing used by a young boy who grew up in Yuma, Arizona in the late 1940s and early 1950s.

The writing style used by the author, a graduate of Arizona State University, is intended to reflect the vernacular of the era of his childhood and his experiences as a native Arizonian born in the great southwest. The obvious misspellings and use of improper grammar are not an oversight, but an intended literary faux pas to give the reader the authentic flavor of life as experienced by the author in a time and place that is now banished to the memories of those who lived it.

Foreword

Cynthia Ozick once said, "Two things are irreversible; time and first impressions." My first impression of "*Riding My Dreams*" spurred me to think of the word *Genuine*. As I carefully read each story, it was easy to see there was nothing faked, fantasized, or untruthful in this collection of personal stories. I say personal stories because I don't feel comfortable labeling this as a memoir. Nor do I believe this technically fits into the genre of an autobiography. However, I can truly say, I thoroughly enjoyed reading each and every story in this collection. By design; the stories in this collection are not in the strict chronological order of a boy who grows up in the great Southwest. However, during his journey along the way to becoming a man, the author pulls the reader right into the life, mind, family, and mentors with his stories. We hear the voice of a child in some of the stories. Yet, as we read further and further into the book; the tone, and reflections of the author, advance along with the stories. The life-lasting virtues picked up along the road to becoming a man are in themselves inspiring. Stories of attaining common sense, reasonable fear, honesty, pride in one's accomplishments, working hard, respect for family, patience, trust, love, and more are infused in every story. Personal ethics and life choices made by the author will leave the reader with a realization of what it means to grow up with a loving family and the help of others along the way. And finally, the author neither pulls punches nor shies away from normally shunned topics while being honest about his feelings towards God, Religion, or other personal beliefs.

Pat Fogarty—Editor and Beta Reader

Contents

On the Road to Yuma

Hard to believe that on a cold Christmas Day at 10:00 in the morning back in 1946 I was born. Yuma General Hospital down in the Yuma Valley on Avenue C was the place of my entry into this world. My father was there to greet me so they say, and his only natural child was given the name Bruce. They never explained that to me. Bruce; where did that come from? I've decided that Yuma was a good place to be born and raised. Equal to all and better than most as they say.

Farmers, ranchers, and rural town folk all make for a fine atmosphere for a boy growing up in America. Away from big city streets, crime, racial hatred, and political bullshit as it came to be known. I had older brothers and a great Mom and Dad. Really fortunate in that aspect of being a boy. They were simple hard-working folk and gave me the ability and encouragement to grow and live free. The story goes that my father said it would be a cold day in hell before he became a father of more children after marrying my mother and adopting my two brothers. It snowed in Yuma on the day I was born. Fascinating, isn't it?

I Remember Jimmy

As a boy in Yuma, I didn't have many friends. Least none I could call on to play with every day or so. One such friend was Jimmy from down the street by my house. He was confined to a wheelchair and couldn't do much in the way of activities. I used to play with my little plastic Indians and Cowboys in the alley behind my house and there was a lot of deep sand there. It was so deep the garbage truck that came down the alley had a hard time with the sand. Jimmy had a hard time also because of the skinny tires on his wheelchair. It was hard for him to go through the sand at all.

That was when the first brainstorm came to me to help Jimmy get through the sand. I had two old bicycle tires hanging on the wall in Dad's shop so I got them and with a bit of a struggle, I got them on over the wheels of Jimmy's wheelchair. This gave him bigger tires and it was a lot easier to go through the sand. The front tires were small and caused us trouble so I tied a board under the front tires to slide on and we were good to go. Together we would act out wars with the Cowboys and the Indians in the sand and we had a great time. Jimmy laughed so hard he started coughing and had to slow down to catch his breath

Mom would call me for lunch and of course, Jimmy came with me. After a sandwich, a cup of soup, and a glass of milk we were ready to get going. I always rinsed off my plate, bowl, and glass. Jimmy asked why I did that and I said it's the rules in mom's kitchen. He wanted to rinse his stuff off as well but he couldn't reach the sink, so I did it for him. I said pals help each other sometimes. Mom asked about the headbands we were wearing and I told her I made them out of old bandanas I found and since we didn't have any feathers we stuck weeds in them instead which we had found in the alley behind the house. We were totally Apache.

I first met Jimmy in 3rd grade which was over at Gila Vista Elementary School. He was always in his wheelchair and the other kids just ignored him when it came time to go to recess. I said I'd push him around and I did every day in school. We got to know each other right away. I would push him out to the end of the playground where they had put up a tin foil barrier to keep the wooly worms out of the schoolyard. He had never before seen a woolly worm and loved playing with them just as much as I did. We would get so wrapped up with them that we would miss the bell to go back to class. We didn't care. One time while out past the bell Jimmy peed his pants and felt bad about it. I told him not to feel so bad I have done it many times. He said his mom would be hurt by his doing so and I said let's go to the restroom and solve the problem. We went there and I dumped water all over his shirt and my shirt and pants as well. Told the teacher we got into a water fight. Problem solved, but we did get in trouble for it.

Out in the dirt lot where the kids would gather to shoot marbles I got Jimmy interested in shooting too. Me and a couple of other guys would drag him out of his chair and put him on the ground. He wore a brace around his back and chest to keep him upright and it was strapped to the back of the wheelchair to keep him from falling. He also had braces on his legs to keep them straight. I unstrapped him and put him on the ground where he could shoot marbles with the rest of us. He wasn't ever very good at marbles but he did like to join in. I remember his mom calling my mom and asking how in the world he got so dirty at school. I told her we would shoot marbles like all the other kids in the dirt. Didn't think much of his mom getting all upset about that. We had a good laugh about it.

Once I was with Jimmy and he said he found something that looked like fun so I pushed him over to where there was a red ant hill. Jimmy said he wanted to play with them and I told him that would not be a good idea cause they will bite you real bad. Jimmy said he had never been bitten before and wanted to try it so he did just that. His mom was really mad this time. My mom got mad too and chewed me out real good. We laughed together later when we talked about it

Jimmy was my age but really skinny and lite, and I could pick him up real easy to put him on the ground or on a swing at school or anywhere really. Mom warned me that Jimmy wasn't a toy to be moved around from chair to ground and back all the time. I told her we were just playing and that I'd be careful with him. As it turns out I was careful but Jimmy wasn't and for some reason couldn't or wouldn't hold on to the swing and fell out several times. Could have killed him but it didn't and he would come up laughing about it and saying let's do it again. I guess I needed a hobby and Jimmy was it, cause we went everywhere together when we could. Jimmy's mom took to me alright but was certain I would hurt Jimmy with our play antics. I never considered hurting my pal cause he was already broke.

Down at the Yuma Theater on Main street every Saturday they held what was called Square Shooters. It was all about kids and we were naturally there every time we could get there. Cokes were a nickel popcorn was 10 cents and getting in was fifty cents to see a western or a serial with Flash Gordon or Gene Autry. Jimmy and I would go as often as his mother would let him and we had a ball. Sometimes I would put him in a seat and take his wheelchair to the side of the theater and sit with him just like good buddies do. His mom would come to get us after the show and of course, she would worry that he was feeling poorly because of all the excitement. We had fun and laughed as hard as we could. I never considered that I was doing Jimmy any harm. We were just being the kids that we were.

Jimmy was really smart at schoolwork, not that 3rd grade was tough or anything, but he could draw really well. He also understood things better than I did and knew the right words to use when speaking. I was very taken with his outlook on things and listened to him very closely. I hoped I too would one day learn to be like Jimmy, and I was sure he would get better and get out of his braces. Told him so cause if you wear a brace long enough your legs will get healed, happens all the time with people in a cast. He said he didn't think it worked like that. I said it had to, so then we could run and play just like the other kids. My mother said I was a dreamer and I took that as a compliment.

Then one day I went to Jimmy's house and his mother said Jimmy could not play today. I told her about going over to the school nearby and swinging and stuff and she said no not today. I asked if he was sick or something and she said Jimmy was tired and needed some rest. I told her I'd check back later to see if he was getting any better. She was crying and told me that Jimmy was sick and may not get better today. I did not understand that at all, but went on home and told my mom about it. She seemed to know a lot more about Jimmy than she ever let on. That's when she told me Jimmy was very weak and not doing well with the medicine he was taking and was in a lot of pain. I told Mom she could tell me all about it cause he was my friend and I needed to know. Mom said when the time was right she would tell me.

I went out and played in the sand with my Cowboys and Indians but it just wasn't the same without Jimmy to play with. I went down to the schoolyard and rode on the swing and climbed around on the monkey bars but it was just no good. A couple of the other kids at the school ground asked where Jimmy was and I told them he wasn't feeling good today. I felt like Jimmy's older brother always looking after him like I did. Missed him when he couldn't come out to play. I Wasn't ready for what happened next.

Jimmy's mom called my mom and said Jimmy was sick and that he couldn't get out of bed. I said I'd be right over and when I got there I was told that Jimmy was asleep and not ready to see anyone. I insisted that he was my pal and I wanted to say hello to him and let him know I was there. Jimmy's mom said alright and took me to Jimmy's bedroom to see him. I could tell he was really tired and he was wearing a mask to get some air. I told Jimmy that playing just wasn't the same without him and that I sure hope he gets better soon. He seemed to smile at me and said he would do the best he can in a very weak voice. That's when Jimmy's mom said I should go now and let Jimmy get his rest.

Later that day at about supper time mom got a call telling her that Jimmy had passed away. I just sat and stared off into space when I heard the news. I don't think I spoke to anyone for a couple of days. I didn't have anything to say. I just didn't know what to say.

That was 65+ years ago and I think about my friend even today. I could go into great detail about what was wrong with Jimmy, but the most vivid memories I have are of the things that were right with Jimmy. I know a bit more about death now than I did back then, but it still cuts deep and long when it happens to our friends and family. I know that friends cause us pain and heartache and even knowing this I haven't stopped making friends. I know for certain that tomorrow is not promised to anyone. We all will pass away from this world sooner or later. I have lost many friends and family along this life's journey. I'm as sure as I can be that I will lose even more before it is over. As it was with my friend Jimmy I will have nothing to say about it and will not know what to say about it. Death is the end of everything a person ever had or ever will have. I just trust that the time Jimmy and I had together while he was alive, were the best days he ever had. I know they were for me.

Here we are in the year 2022 and I have just achieved the glorious age of 75 years last Christmas. It has been a marvelous journey so far in this life. Seen a lot of things I never thought I'd see. Been a lot of things I never thought I'd be. Mostly I have lived longer than I ever dreamed I would live, and all of that with a mind that still wonders about what will come next. Have come to the decision that what will be . . .will be. The good Lord knows what is in store for me and mine and He isn't letting on about it. Just as well, I probably couldn't handle it any better knowing it was coming as I will when it gets here. We have time in our lives and that serves us well so that everything doesn't happen all at once.

I'm the last of the Yuma Sparks family, and I'm all right with that. My older brother Billy once told me no matter what happens to me in life, just put dirt on it and don't tell Mom. Sage advice from the man I looked up to all of my boyhood days. As life often is for me, others have put dirt on my accomplishments and my failures, and not telling Mom was always the rule.

My father was like an oak tree of manhood to me. Strong and always busy doing what he needed to do to make a home and a covering over the rest of us. I used to think he was the locomotive that pulled our train as a family. Sitting at the dinner table, smoking his pipe and drinking coffee, getting ready for the next load he would pull to keep us on track. Mom cleaning and cooking, cleaning and cooking, seemed she never stopped to take a break from doing her chores. Church on Sunday was most always morning and night. Prayer meeting on Wednesday night, and quilting bees on Fridays. Visiting missionaries were always part of the scene and staying at our home was most likely for them. My father was not a church-going man. He always said those church-going Baptists were one-eyed jacks and he had seen the other side of them.

I was a slow reader in school and at home. Always behind in following the schoolteacher and the rest of the class on reading and doing the school work. Didn't like being the last to learn or the one called on in class that did not know the answer to the problem. I didn't even know what the problem was let alone the answer. School for me did not hold the allure it seemed to hold for the other kids. I just wanted out and spent my time daydreaming about where I could be and what I could be doing.

It was clear to me at an early age that I was sent to school to be watched and babysat all day so that my parents didn't have to. I was expected to conform and be like all the other kids in their contentment with life in the classroom. I didn't disrupt the classroom nor did I speak out against the norm. I just didn't give a darn about what was being handed to me as education. All through my childhood I was often asked what I wanted to be when I grew up, and I would always respond "an adult." Whatever came around would be fine for me. One decade into this life I knew in Yuma, I got to be around horses and learn what they could bring to me in my young life. I had found I was able to begin my acceptance of being part of a world larger than the one I had known. Going to rodeos and being with my brother Billy almost all of the time were the building blocks of what I was to become. Rodeo was opening my eyes to see what could happen to one if given the opportunity to try hard to get good at something. Getting good at something you liked was the key to success.

A line from my favorite movie "Chinatown" resonated with me when I heard it for the first time, "Come on Jake, it's Chinatown.." indicating that what takes place here is all because of where it is and who the people are. Yuma was like Chinatown to me at an early age. I blamed what was happening in my life on the town I lived in, the people of that town, and the way we lived back then. In reality, it had nothing to do with Yuma or the people. It was me all along and the way my mind worked--or didn't work. It all began with a horse out on my uncle's place in the Gila Valley. It's a simple story about a boy learning about life and death up close and personal. From this humble beginning with a horse, I was soon to learn about happiness, hurt, disapproval, and acceptance. A good way to start for a boy with no real aspirations or expectations.

Ω

Cowboys and Indians
5 or 6 Years Old

In my father's house, I used to sit on a rug in the middle of the floor by myself and play with a set of small molded plastic Cowboys and Indians. Some of them were red and some yellow. Some of them had horses and some just stood on the concrete floor. They wouldn't sit on the rug with me because of the rough surface, but they would stand on the cold concrete floor beside me and I would enter a world of make-believe with them for hours on end.

As the time went past I would play with my little friends, and sometimes the Indians would win the battle, and sometimes the Cowboys would be the winners. I didn't keep score of who won and who lost. It wasn't important at the time to even things out and have balance in the games I would play. There were no favorites and there were no leaders. At the end of the day, they all went in a shoebox together that I kept under my bed. There under my bed, they were hidden away and safe and I knew they were there waiting for me to take them out again.

Then one day for whatever reason, I lost interest in playing with my little friends. Other things in life took me away from the games I would play with them. Maybe it was boredom that took me away from them, or maybe just moving on to other things and interests. They stayed under my bed waiting for me to return and I thought of them often but never came back.

As I think about those times now so many years later, I can see them in that box under the bed waiting for me. I wish I had them now and could see them and hold them again. It was a simpler time in why life and I want to recapture it now that the years have come and gone. Now that my values have been changed in the way I see the world. I would like to go back again and sit on the floor in my father's house and just play with my little friends and find peace and contentment. I would love to block out all the hurtful things that prey on my mind because of what I have done and what I have endured.

All of life's trials and tribulations. Everything that has gone on that has shaped and molded me. Every heartbreak, every loss, and every sad event could be removed with a simple set of little plastic figures to play with on the floor.

But then they are always with me in my mind. I can see them clearly right now standing here and ready to take me away. All I have to do is sit and clear my mind for a moment and they appear from under the bed in that old shoebox. I'm going on a trip with them and see if things will look better in the morning. I believe they can make a difference. I believe they already have.

Kings

Across the street from our house at 763 S Orange Avenue, in Yuma, Arizona, was the Connor Tire Company, on the North West Corner of Orange Avenue and 8th Street. Connor Tire was the repair place for the trucks that came out of the produce fields in both valleys north and south of Yuma, those being the Yuma Valley and the Gila Valley. We never knew when a truck from the fields would pull in with a tire problem but it happened a lot during the summers in Yuma. I must have been 5 years old at that time but it seems as clear to me today as it was some 60-plus years ago.

Any time a truck with melons would pull in for tire repair to that place of business, it was often loaded with melons from the fields. That's when my brothers Billy and Jimmy would go into action. Jimmy was the brains of the outfit and Billy was the muscle. Working as a team one would climb into the bed of the truck and throw a melon down to the other and he would pitch it off to the side of the parking lot through a hedge so they would not be seen. Before you knew it several large beautiful melons or a bunch of fresh cantaloupe would be offloaded from the truck and the boys would disappear till the truck left after getting the needed repair. Once the scene was clear of anything happening at the tire place the boys would scurry over to where the melons were and collect the bounty in an old wheelbarrow. With one as the lookout when the coast was clear, the other would wheel the load of melons into our backyard right across the street.

The next order of business was ice and that was down at Third Street and Ninth Avenue at Yuma Ice Company. 50 Cents bought more than enough ice for their needs and home. They would come with the Ice for the melons. Making the melons cold was a real treat to watch for the imaginative brothers. With the melons in a tub full of water and ice, they would fire up Dad's evaporative cooling shop fan and aim it at the tub. On those days when getting Ice was not possible, they would wrap the melons in a wet gunny sack and do the evaporative fan the same way. Before you could say stolen bounty the melons were ready to sell and sell they did. With a big hand-painted sign and curbside service, the boys would sell the melons as fast as the cars came by. Slices of cold melon for $.25 and they would sell out faster than anything on a hot summer day.

Money for Movies, Sodas, Popcorn, and of course Candy was the goal and they did it every time they got the chance. All my life I have been told crime doesn't pay, but I can tell you for a fact it does pay, and very well. Nobody knew how they got the melons, nobody cared how they got the melons and after selling the produce was over the evidence was gone. My older brothers were the Kings of Orange Avenue at selling cold watermelon and cantaloupe. And I was right there to see it all.

Old Pen

8 Years Old

Standing in the sun on a hot May day. That's how I remember seeing old Pen in the corral for the first time. He was snoozing in the heat and the flies were everywhere. My job was to care for him and give him some exercise around the place. How to feed, how to water, and how to groom all came with the territory, and I was to learn every part of it and how to muck out his stall.

Must have spooked him 'cause the first time he saw me he was a bit shaken and bolted across the corral. Seemed very spry for a horse well past the age of 25 years. His hooves had been cleaned recently and his nails trimmed. Took me a while to realize what it meant to go barefoot but Pen had not worn shoes in many a year. Seems he did not have anyone to ride him very much, if at all. That was part of my job also when the time came. Time in this case was for me to muster up the sand to get up on Pen if I could. I needed to figure out how horses allow people to get up on them and the trust they have that it will be good for both parties. That was going to be a bit further down the trail for me and I was content to stay on the ground for now.

Pen was a mix of gray and gold with a dark strip running down his back. His mane and tail were darker as was his face. Above his eyes and on his face there were patches of gray. I remember Uncle Fergie calling him a dun Horse. Pen had been a very good roping horse in his day and as a younger man with Pen, Uncle Fergie said he was a lot better than most other ropers.

Pen let me walk up to him and stroke his neck, but he would not come to me at all. I reckon he didn't know me that well, and it would take some time for him to know why I was there. It was up to me to show him what I could do for him. Learning how to brush and curry was part of the job, but that came later as well. The first order of business, according to my Uncle Fergie, was to clean out Pen's stall. I was a natural for that according to him and I took readily to being praised for being a quick study.

Every day it seemed for a week or so I was introduced to another part of the job about the care of Pen. Pen was an older horse and he needed help with his feed. I learned to soak his feed in warm water before giving it to him; his ability to chew hay was not good anymore. In the heat of that summer,

Pen drank a lot of water every day and I made sure he had fresh water to drink. In about two to three weeks we were getting to know each other, and Pen stopped trying to step on my feet every time he got the chance. A carrot or an apple won his affection more than any other thing I could do.

Pen had a fly mask that he wore but it needed to be sewn up a bit. I made sure that I did the repair job in front of him so he could see that I was doing something for him. Once completed it fit better and did a better job of keeping the flies away from his eyes. As time went on I found that keeping his stall clean made a difference in the number of flies around the place. There were other horses in other stalls but the people that boarded them there kept them cleaned up and were at the place almost daily. One of the ranch hands was in charge of a front-end loader for picking up the manure from the horses and hauling it off, so it was a pretty smoothly run operation. Regarding the horse droppings in general, I soon learned the advantage of having boots to wear instead of tennis shoes. Uncle Fergie gave me a pair of rubber boots to wear and for a boy walking in horse droppings every day they were great.

Pen got to trusting me in time. Don't know if he ever took a liking to me. He liked going for walks down the dirt road that led to the levee and the runoff from the Laguna Diversion Dam. Big salt cedars were everywhere down there and that meant snakes among other things. Pen didn't get spooked very easily around such critters, but he did let me know when one was around. I soon learned to pay attention to his warnings.

From the heat of May, June, and July and on into the more humid heat of August, we spent almost every day together. Didn't have school to contend with and was thinking about how this job would work when school did get back in session. Had a few more weeks to figure that out, but for now, it was time I started riding Pen. Had some tack in the tack room for him but I didn't know how to work it. So with nothing more than a handful of mane and the corral fence to be up on, I went aboard. Getting down wasn't hard at all but getting back up without the fence was not possible.

Pen understood the problem for me and he had a solution. He bent down with his front legs and then with his hind legs. I had no problem at all climbing on board. Then he would stand up and away we would go. For an animal that did not speak, he sure could communicate. I will never know the why of his actions except to say he understood what I wanted to do and he made it happen. From then on riding was no problem for me and Pen.

I learned about horses and their need to sleep. Pen didn't need a long timeout as he would lay down to sleep, but a few hours did him some real good I could tell. Other than his getting down, he would rest most of the day if I wasn't bothering him.

One day the vet showed up to look at Pen and his teeth. I did not know about such things and learned that horses needed a dentist just like we do from time to time. The vet took blood samples and waited for Pen to pee so he could get some urine to test. About every six weeks the farrier came to trim his nails and Pen seemed to like that a lot. Horses and their care were beginning to be part of my world. Heck, I might even turn out to be a horseman or maybe a rodeo rider of some sort.

Riding was just walking and always bareback as Pen didn't care for saddles or bridles. Me and old Pen would be just walking down the road and nobody seemed to care at all. Our time in the sun was ours alone and no others. Pen loved for me to turn the water hose on him and cool him off in the shade. Uncle Fergie said I needed to use some sort of headstall to control Pen like when he needed to stop or turn. He talked to me like I knew what he was talking about so I said that I would do that. Wasn't hard to figure out how to use the hackamore and we then used it all the time.

The things I learned from Pen and with him would carry me through many times and trials in my life. I didn't want to leave Pen without his knowing why I was not going to be coming to see him every day. School was about to start and that meant I'd be spending my days in school and not seeing him. When I told Uncle Fergie about my school starting up, he said that would be it for Pen. He said that would be fine, he would deal with it, and off I went. Never occurred to me that Pen, at his advanced years, was still alive because of me and the care I gave him.

I started school and stopped going to see Pen. Must've been Christmas break before I had any time to go out to the valley to see my old friend. Had to depend on Mom and Dad to take me out there of course, and when I got there Pen was gone. I looked all over the place and could not find him. His tack was gone and his stall was cleaned out and not being used.

Mom and Dad seemed to know something that I didn't when Uncle Fergie said Pen was gone. I remember Uncle Fergie talking to my father about blood in Pen's urine and the vet telling him it was going to be expensive. Fergie said the practical side of him had to overcome the sentimental side when it came to Pen. In the conversation, I heard the word "useless" being used. Along with that was the fact that Pen was going to turn 30 years old in January.

I was learning about words in school that sometimes run together to convey meaning. One of those words was "worthless," to me meaning something was worth less than something else. But in my mind something still had value. I found it odd that not everybody sees it the same way.

Fergie's ranch, Fergie's animals, Fergie's business, and I was not a partner in it like I thought I was. It has often been said in my life that learning has not occurred until behavior changes. Some things we just don't want to learn. Some things we just don't want to change. I made up my mind right then that any behavior changes in me would be determined by me and no one else from then on if I could make it happen that way.

Wasn't until many years later I understood the meaning of blood in the urine of an older, past-his-prime horse. That, along with teeth issues and his inability to eat well, and weight loss spelled the end for Pen. The biggest part of everything was the fact that Pen was old and worn out. I have often thought maybe I could have done more for him when I was there every day, but those are the thoughts we have with everyone and every animal that passes away from us.

I wasn't with him when he passed but I was a devoted fan of his for one long hot summer there in Yuma. Turns out it was Pen's last summer to spend with a boy that really did learn about the care and feeding of an animal. My first summer to care for an animal and to learn about his life. I have never been one to give my affection easily, it has to be won. Pen taught me that because he did just that. I am proud to say Pen was a teacher to me and he was my friend.

Somewhere there is a ledger of the things we learn early on in our lives. Some of these things stay with us and others fall away from our collective memory. It might be that we hold on to the memories we have because we need them to help us along the way. Maybe they are just so strong that they will not fade away. Could be they are just the best we can have to live on in our minds. I believe they are a little bit of all of these things.

Ω

Con Pelo's

8-years-old

"Tuve que ganarme las espuelas todos los dias"

I had to earn my spurs every day as a boy in Yuma.

Writing a story about being a child in a man's world in Yuma. There were critters to be dealt with and my Uncle Fergi called these critters Cow Killers Asesinos de Vacas. The Mexicans around that area and the ones that worked for Uncle Fergi called them Hormiga con Pelos. These in actuality as I found out much later were called Velvet Ants but the Mexicans working there at the time apparently could not say Terciopelo which is Spanish for Velvet or did not know that word for these critters. If they did they did not use it and said Hormiga con Pelos meaning Ants with Hair. These critters were very aggressive and would hurt anyone and anybody for any reason at any time. The female is the one that crawls around and is a nuisance to the animals. It is a form of a wasp and the male is the one with wings. Getting in the feed and being picked up in the mouth of a cow or horse would sting and cause the throat to close up thereby causing death without aid from the humans in attendance if any. These are the stories I was told about these critters. I did not firsthand witness the death of a horse or cow during my many days out and around the livestock out on Uncle Fergi's place in the Gila Valley north of Yuma.

Yuma seems like a foreign country to me these many years later.

Buenos Suerte

Justin

10 years old

I first met Wayne at Don's place through my brother Billy. Billy, being a member of the Junior Chamber of Commerce Mounted Posse, owned a horse by the name of Duke that he boarded at Don's place. Duke was a small horse for Billy, who was 6-foot-4 and just over 200 pounds. Duke was a curiosity to me 'cause he only had one testicle. Now why and how this fact came to be known to a 10-year-old boy in the first place is still a mystery to me some 60 years later.

Wayne was a man who had been around horses all his life. His knowledge of horse problems and their cures was always reliable and sound. But he was a drinking man and when on the juice, which happened from time to time, he was mean both to people and to animals.

Wayne owned a horse named Justin, a sorrel gelding with a lot of red in his mane and tail which seemed to be on fire. Justin was the largest horse I had ever seen in my life. He stood tall even for Wayne, who was 6-foot-5. Wayne had to reach up to grab the horn on the saddle to mount him. I was told Justin was a fine roping horse 'cause he was strong and quick from a jump.

The first time I got close to Justin he looked me over real good and wanted me to touch him. He sniffed around my head and neck as I rubbed his nose and stroked his neck. I felt like we would be together till the bitter end, he and I. Funny how those thoughts can come back to haunt you later. I liked Justin and I sensed that he liked me, too.

Don had several head of horses and was always looking for an extra hand to help feed, water, ride, and clean up after them. I would ride my bicycle down to Don's place to work with the horses. I didn't know a thing about these animals, but I was willing to learn and not afraid of hard work.

Wayne and Don worked together in the horse business and made it a practice of meeting often to work the horses and discuss buying and selling. Don, as president of the Yuma Jaycees, Junior Chamber of Commerce, was in charge of several other members of the Jaycees' horses that boarded at his place.

Soon I was introduced to an eight-year-old chestnut mare named Zona. I thought, because of being in Arizona, that was a fitting name for her. She was beautiful with a light-colored mane and tail, and very gentle to be around, especially for a kid who knew nothing about horses contrary to popular opinion, a horse will intentionally step on a person and think it's the thing to do. I learned this right away with Zona and soon it became a ritual for her to try to step on me, and for me to avoid getting stepped on. I learned to wash, curry, and brush her, even to clean her hooves. I learned first and foremost how to clean out stalls and change water and feed. Zona was very tolerant of me and I of her. On her, I learned how to sit in a saddle, and how to control a horse and ride. It took months for me to gather this all in and understand the why of it all.

Zona was fun to ride but she had a game she liked to play. When nearing a fence or post of any kind, she would intentionally walk close so as to drag my leg against the object. I thought for some time that she couldn't see well. Once I figured it out, I would just rein her straight into the fence or post. She would give it a wide berth rather than bang her head. She could see just fine. I learned in that short time that horses don't forget things, and they can sense meanness in a person. I was not a mean person with animals, and I didn't know enough about horses to show fear.

Don had a stallion there named Patch who was said to be very mean to everyone--just because he could be. He never seemed to bother me while I was mucking out his stall. Then someone told me that males don't like to stay in a stall with their own droppings, unlike females who will stand in poop all day long and think nothing of it. So if I didn't keep the stall clean, Patch would kick his droppings out all over the place and act mean. I guess because of my age and the fact that I posed no threat to Patch, he let me do almost anything with him and to him. I could water him down on a hot day, brush him, comb him, clean his hooves, and walk him around.

The one thing Don told me not to do is to try and ride him. He said that might be the end of me as a human being if I tried. I hadn't thought much about being a human being prior to that and I took the 'no ride Patch' thing as a challenge. I mean, he was my friend and I did things for him that he seemed to like, right?

One day when I was feeling particularly full of spit and vinegar and bored with the chores I was doing, I walked Patch out to the pasture. While hanging on to the hackamore he wore, I swung myself aboard and expected the worst from him. Patch didn't do a thing, so I gave him some heel. All he did was walk around with me on him like it was nothing. I leaned right, he'd go right. I leaned left, he'd go left. I leaned back, he'd stop.

This was not the excitement I thought I was getting into when I jumped up on his back. I got off and walked around in front of him. He looked at me while shaking his head up and down, with a look that I can only describe as "You are my friend." I had made a connection with an animal and I didn't even know how or why. I did love that horse. From then on wherever I went Patch would follow me. I could ride him anytime I wanted with no problem at all.

Then one day Patch wasn't there anymore. Don had sold him and my friend was gone. Something I wanted with all my heart, in my short life, was taken away from me and it wasn't even mine to have. I couldn't even say "No, you can't do that." I was devastated over the loss and my two years of working with horses came to a stop. I put Zona and the others out of my mind and moved on with my life without even slowing down. Billy and I talked it over, and he came up with an idea. In Little Britches Rodeo, I would ride horses that I didn't know for eight seconds at a time, and then walk away from them if I could. Rodeo was my way of putting distance between me and the animals I loved.

I think about that black horse and the bond we made more and more these days. Maybe it's my age or maybe it's the need to remember pure, sweet days with a true friend. A friend that knows you for the person you are and responds with all they have. Every boy needs to have a friend that is true. Then he will know for sure those who aren't and give them as little of his time as possible. Don said the sale of the black horse was strictly business and I shouldn't concern myself with it. I have lived my life with people who have said that to me. It's business and not personal, you need to learn that.

Then there was the day that put a lid on my time with horses for the rest of my life. My brother Billy and I went over to see Wayne for some reason or another. I can't even remember now the reason for our visit. When we got to Wayne's place we saw Justin on the passenger side of Wayne's truck, kicking the crap out of the side of the truck with both back legs. I could clearly see a pitchfork sticking out of Justin's right hip. It was in pretty deep and bleeding a lot. The handle had been broken off and only the metal was visible, but it had to have been in his hip about five to six inches and was very painful for him.

Justin was on fire about the deal and had snot flowing out of his mouth and nose. His back hooves were bleeding from kicking the truck. I could tell this ordeal had been going on for some time as Justin seemed to be getting weaker as he went. Then we heard Wayne yelling for help from under the truck.

Billy told me to try and get Justin away from the truck if I could and he would see about Wayne from the other side. Justin took an interest in us and came for us hell-bent on making us aware of his situation. Billy threw up his hands and started waving his arms and yelling at Justin to stop. But when that horse reared up on his bloody back legs and hooves, he appeared to reach for the sky. I swear he looked 20 feet tall. I know he didn't recognize us. That's when Billy and I ran for cover. I don't know why Justin came my way as I was running, but I knew I had to get on something or under something fast. I went under the rail fence beside the pasture.

Justin stopped at that point and just snorted in my direction. I could see he was bleeding from the mouth pretty badly and had several scrapes and gouges down both sides of his neck and shoulders, which were also bleeding. Justin stood there for what seemed like the longest time just looking at me, the same way he had looked at me the first time I met him. He seemed to say "Who are you and what do you want?" Billy by that time had gotten to Wayne and dragged him out from under the truck. The next thing I knew, Billy was driving Wayne's truck out onto the highway as fast as he could with Wayne in the truck with him. Justin was almost tuckered out from all the excitement and loss of blood, no doubt.

I walked down the fence line toward the house and Justin walked slowly with me on the other side of the fence. I could see where he had gone through the fence, apparently on his way to go after Wayne, and I suspected the pitchfork in his hip was not an accident. I wanted to help him but I also knew he was hurt. Did your Daddy ever tell you not to get too close to a hurt animal? I sure wasn't about to reach out to Justin right now. Even if I meant him no harm, I wasn't so sure he felt that way about me or anybody.

I worked my way into Wayne's house and called my Dad. He said he'd be there soon as he could. I gave him directions and of course, told him about Justin and Wayne. Justin was over by the corral, just standing there breathing hard and bleeding. I kept out of sight from him and waited for Dad to get there. Dad drove into the drive very slowly and came up to the house. I met him outside the front door and showed him where Justin was.

He could see the horse was in serious trouble so he went in and phoned a veterinarian he had known for years. It wasn't long 'til the vet got there and looked the situation over. A Sheriff's Deputy was also on the scene as the vet had called them about being there to care for an injured animal without the owner being present. Things were getting complicated, but no help for Justin had been given yet. The Deputy had a Winchester with him and said he'd put the animal down if he got out of control. I didn't want to tell him the war was over and Justin won. The vet then approached Justin with two syringes full of horse tranquilizers.

Justin seemed played out 'cause he just stood there and let the vet stick him with both needles. Maybe his pain was so great he didn't feel them. Soon he was down and vet and the deputy pulled the fork out of his hip, with considerable effort I might add. Both rear hooves were split and busted, his shoulders and neck were cut pretty deep, and cuts around his mouth were pretty bad. All in all, Justin had taken a lot of injuries to get at Wayne for what we all knew was pure drunken meanness.

It turns out Wayne had been drinking and, as usual, was feeling mean and hateful. I guess he had gotten into it a bit with Justin over something in the corral. One thing led to another, and Justin got the pitchfork in the hip. Then Wayne got Justin's mouth over his right shoulder. Justin had bit Wayne deep and hard. Justin's front teeth came down the front of Wayne's chest while Justin's lower teeth went down Wayne's back. The bite was deep and long, tore a lot of muscle, and pulled bones out of place, breaking a few.

Wayne had lost a lot of blood by the time Billy got him to the hospital, but they saved him for a short while. Wayne's wounds became septic and within about three days he died. He didn't have much of a liver anyway from hitting the bottle so often and long, so old Justin really did him in.

The County Sheriff by court order went a step further with the situation. The death certificate for Wayne listed the cause of death as injuries and accompanying trauma sustained by an animal attack. Seems when an animal causes the death of a human, no matter what the provocation, the animal is doomed.

Billy and I were at Wayne's place cleaning up after the animals and caring for them as best we could when the Sheriff came to take Justin away. They brought a horse trailer and wanted to load him up and take him on his final ride. They were very clear that they had all the court documents and legal papers with them to do what they were about to do.

Billy and I were amazed that they would even talk about how right they were when that horse had done only what he could do, go after the man that had hurt him. Justin, being all banged up and bruised, was in no condition to fight a normal fight, but he wasn't going without giving them all he had in protest. He knew those men meant to do him harm and he wanted no part of their paper serving, nor any ride anywhere.

As long as I live I will never understand the ending of a life for spite. Wayne died because he was cruel to Justin. Now Justin must die because he defended himself against cruelty. I watched those men shoot Justin and kill him. The bitter end had indeed come and I was there with him till then.

Just before they shot Justin he walked over to me and looked into my very soul. I touched him and rubbed his nose while he sniffed all around my face. I felt small, I felt hurt, I felt pain, and most of all I felt a kinship with him that only he and I could feel. Billy said it was the strangest thing he had ever seen Justin do.

Some say horses are really smart and act a lot like humans from being around humans for so long. I say they will steal your heart and your dreams about life faster than any woman I have ever known. Broken hearts about women will mend. Broken dreams about horses live forever.

I still remember Justin and his way of dealing with what he was given as his lot in life. Through him, I learned a very valuable lesson about doing the right thing, even at the cost of your life. He had taken all he was going to take from a cruel person, he did what he felt he had to do, yet he remembered me and showed me his gentleness and friendship. Justin will live in my heart forever.

Changing Direction

After my dealing with Justin, I was devastated and needed to move in a new direction. My brother Billy convinced me to try my hand at rodeo. It wasn't a far reach for me, I still wanted to be around horses. I just didn't want the pain they can bring by breaking your heart. Instead, I went for the pain they can bring by breaking your bones. Billy said this would be a way to stay in the game of riding horses but with the reward that goes with being good at it. I wasn't good at the start and that brought no reward, but I got better every time I tried.

It was a fast learning curve riding broncs. I tried bareback riding and saddle bronc riding and liked the saddle bronc the best. Billy was a roper and had taken very well to the rigors of riding and roping, plus he had a very smart and quick horse. Billy was my idol back then and I wanted to prove myself to him by doing good. Doing good meant winning. Billy was a winner and I wanted to be like him. Billy was five years older than I and had been doing rodeo roping for a few years. He had a steady day job so turning pro in rodeo was not his desire. I didn't think about my future at that time. I just lived for the moment.

In and around Yuma, my hometown, there were many opportunities to try our luck at riding and roping. Seems there were a lot of folks with rough stock and they were always having get-togethers for men and boys to try their hand at learning how not to ride a rank horse. Roping events were held almost weekly that Billy could get into. I got to practice a lot; it was fun and not in front of a big crowd. Failure comes at a price to your ego I soon learned. You either suck it up and go on with it or you quit. I was not raised to be a quitter. Winning comes at a cost and that cost is pain: physical, mental, and emotional.

A few things I would point out at this time was how I was not outfitted for doing this activity. My folks bought clothes they could afford for us kids. I never had a pair of Levi's or Wrangler brand trousers, and the ones I did have were not made well and tore easily due in no small part to being made cheaply and of thin material. Didn't have any Western shirts, belts, or boots, and had to get me some or not be able to compete. I learned to ride in tight, stiff Levi's 501 button-fly jeans. Like wearing armor to me and I liked it.

Quality belts and the buckles that go with them were highly sought after in the small-town rodeo world I was living in. Turns out they are still sought after in the big town rodeo world, and even more so. I needed boots to do this riding thing so I bought a pair of boots from a Mexican boot maker there in Yuma. They fit me like a glove and wore like armor, just like my stiff and rugged Levi's. The man who made those boots gave me a pair of spurs to wear in my chosen line of sport. I wore them often till I figured out they were too long a shank for me. I wore those boots for many years after my rodeo days were over.

Boots have always been my choice of footwear over the years cause you never know when you will get the opportunity to throw your leg over another bronc and let 'er rip into the arena in search of glory in the sun. Boots also beat the heck out of tennis shoes when it comes to stepping in horse poop, and that happens a lot if you don't watch where you're stepping.

It was 1960--I was 13 years old and not willing to sit on the fence and watch other boys ride when I decided to give this rodeo thing a try. Had me some cheap jeans and a pair of hand-me-down hiking boots to start out with. Borrowed a bareback rig from another contestant and figured without a saddle and stirrups I would do better at this thing called bronc riding. My brother drilled me beforehand on the rules of the sport. Spur out first thing and keep it going or be disqualified, no touching nothing with your free hand or be disqualified, and if you need to quit before the buzzer, don't do it 'cause you will be disqualified.

It seemed pointless for Billy to tell me that I needed to go where the horse went, but as it turns out, that is exactly where the success in this sport is. Going where the horse isn't is the horse's desire for you and you will fail in your attempt to ride. Staying with him during your ride is the key to riding to the buzzer. I found out early that I liked the saddle and stirrups better than bareback. An old friend of my father had a saddle rig and it was a good one. I told him of my plans to ride broncs and he asked if my father was aware of my plans. I told him no and that I would sure appreciate him not telling anyone about this, especially my father. He said he would not tell so I bought the rig. Regarding not telling my father, the man did not keep his word.

Yuma, Somerton, Wellton, Bard, and as far away as Wickenburg and Prescott there were many chances for me to hone my skills. I worked at it very hard for several months and got better as I went. Looking forward to getting to a bigger arena and more horses came much sooner than I had expected. I wanted to prove to myself that I could do this thing and do it the best I could.

In October of 1961 Billy and I went to Brawley, California for The Brawley Cattle Call Rodeo and I won my first silver rodeo buckle. I also got cut on the chin pretty bad and had to have stitches. I was so proud of that buckle that I thought I was going to bust and never really paid attention to my chin. Billy was doing good with his roping and won first place for timed roping. That meant good money for him and he was very happy about the whole event.

My mother on the other hand was very concerned about my injury and it was the first--so she said--she had heard about my riding efforts. Billy had always told me, "If you get hurt, just rub dirt on it and don't tell Mom." That rubbing dirt part was easy. The other part about not telling Mom about rodeo wasn't easy. Mom was hurt about me keeping my sporting adventures from her. She believed that by not telling her what I was doing I was lying. I tried to use the line about not wanting to hurt her or make her worry. She didn't buy it. I cried when I realized I had hurt her. My father said I was trying to grow up way too fast.

Looking back I think the tears gave me away as a boy trying to do manly things. The other part was my excitement at winning a prize I equated to doing right and being good enough. Seemed at that time in my life no one cared about that shiny, silver buckle as much as I did. My mother prayed that I would see the light and stop putting myself in harm's way as she saw it. I felt like a prisoner on parole. I wanted to do the right thing but was all balled up inside over which way to go. Whatever I decided I would have to stick to it and own up to it if I was wrong. Billy always said to go for it and don't look back. He also told me those girls at the events in those skin-tight Wranglers don't have any more going for themselves in the brains category than I did. He was so right.

Billy had a 1949 International pickup truck and it always seemed to need mechanical attention for one thing and another. Dad was helping Billy with it one day and saw my saddle rig in the truck bed. He made a comment about his days trying to do the very same thing. It was the first time I ever knew he did what I was doing. Sometimes we find out firsthand that the apple does not fall far from the tree.

After that, I kept on doing the riding thing but didn't talk about it at home. I started to see the logic of my not telling Mom about what I was doing. What she did not know would not hurt her. Years later I found out she knew about my exploits all along and at the insistence of my father never mentioned it. I thought my rebellion was unique and all my own doing. Turns out one of my biggest fans and supporters was my father. His job was to keep my mother from stopping me in my quest for fame and fortune. As it turned out, fame and fortune never did come my way. I thought I wanted it but I guess I didn't want it bad enough.

In the years I was active in rodeo, my father never talked about his part in my desire to be a somebody. He seemed to like hearing about my ups and downs but never said whether he was for me or not. The last buckle I won was to me the best of all the ones before. I gave that buckle to my father. He said he would hold onto it for me as one day I would like to have it back and I'd always know where it was. Dad was my silent partner.

1960 through 1964 I wore spurs to make my way into the man's world I wanted to be in. I got pretty good at bronc riding--at least my buckle collection would attest to that. Then I hung up my spurs and put on a flight suit. The US Navy was my next arena, and I became a flight crew member of Patrol Squadron 28 stationed out of Barbers Point Naval Air Station, Hawaii. I have always said learning has not occurred until behavior changes. That was never more apparent to me until I experienced the change from the smell of horse manure to the smell of aviation fuel. There were no buckles being given out in the Navy; they gave out wings of gold. But just like those rodeo buckles, you had to earn them. The earning of those wings came at a cost which I was willing to pay.

Fifty-eight years later now and it is still the same: no one cares about those buckles at all. I don't even wear those buckles to hold my pants up, but I earned them and I am still proud to have done that. The last buckle I won was as a Senior Cowboy in Little Britches Rodeo. I was 17 years old at the time and figured my rodeoing days were coming to an end. I was getting good at it according to my brother and a few friends. I guess it was time to move on to other challenges in my life. That buckle was the best of all I had and the end of a time in my life I love to reach back to and remember.

I got that favorite buckle back after Dad passed away. Mom gave it to me with a note that was attached to it. She told me Dad kept it in the drawer by his chair and would sit and hold it often as he drank his coffee. He told her it was the light of the sun for him and he loved to have it. When I read the note Dad had written, I cried like a little boy. In his difficult-to-read scribble, I made out these words:

"I don't have the words to say thank you near enough.
You have been my inspiration whenever things got tough.
Thanks for the loan, it meant a lot, sure is pretty in the sun.
When it comes to winning buckles boy—You are number one.
Love,
Dad"

You can bet I kept that note from Dad, and the buckle is still my pride and joy. Not for how or when I got it but for it bringing joy to my father. That is something I take great pride in.

Direction change in my life has happened many times. Some of them I made on my own; some were made by others for me. I always say I have three Bachelor's Degrees given out by women I have known. I have never considered myself to be fortunate or gifted. What I have found is that I have overcome failure time after time due in no small part to learning how and how not to ride horses, and how to pick myself up off the ground when I failed. I thank God for that ability, and for *Him* watching over me all those years.

Ω

Sandy Girl

Going to high school in Yuma for me was a time of being ordinary and of blending into the wallpaper to not be noticed. It was my time in the rodeo arena with my brother Billy and no one around me in school knew what I did. I never wore boots to school. Clothes like Western shirts and belts with buckles denoting rodeo were not my dress code. I never spoke about what I did when I was away from school to anyone. When I would see some of the kids from school at the events I attended, I would just ignore them 'cause they did not know me. Even if they heard my name over the speaker it would mean nothing to them.

My brother Billy was known by many in the area as a very skilled roper and rodeo personality, but the connection to me was not part of that. It never occurred to me that some girls were attracted to rodeo performers and I personally never experienced any of that. I would say that seeing those cowgirls in skin-tight Wranglers was enough to drive any boy to risk life and limb on a wild horse.

In my years as a young aspiring saddle bronc rider from 1960 to 1964, I won several buckles and gained in my ability to ride, getting better as I went along. My brother was always there to encourage me and care for me when I got hurt. "Put dirt on it and don't tell Mom." He was quick to celebrate with me when I won. I, in turn, supported Billy in his roping and took extra care of his horse for him when he could not.

We practiced a lot and it seems we were always playing in the dirt with horses for most, if not all, of my high school years. Wasn't fame I was seeking but acceptance in the world I had found with my brother. Turns out acceptance is something we have to find inside ourselves and it comes after a lot of trial and error. Acceptance is always found to the degree to which we want to be accepted. The key to acceptance is how hard we work for it and to what extent we are willing to put it all on the line to find it. I did what I was told to do and practiced all the time to get better.

During my years at KOFA High School, also from 1960 to 1964, I was really taken by a girl that did not know I was even on this planet. Cheerleader, Drama Club, Pep Squad—high society in every way. Her name was Sandy and she was beautiful. Sandy's hair was always done well and she wore the perfect outfits. Her makeup was done exceptionally well, she had a great smile and she was an all-around gorgeous girl. Very popular and known by all, she was a girl I could never approach 'cause I was a nobody and not active in anything to do with school.

I was gone on weekends with my brother practicing and going to various events in and around the state, sometimes skipping school to attend events. I do not recall if Sandy was ever in any of my classes. I'm not sure to this day, but I am fairly confident in saying that I never once ever spoke to her about anything. For some reason, I knew she was a farm girl but if she had a boyfriend, if she rode the bus, if she drove a car, if she was involved in sports, I just did not know.

Strange to think that a boy and a girl in the same school for several years never spoke to each other, especially when the boy was infatuated with the girl. Things could easily have changed in both of our lives if I had taken the lead in getting to know her. I was more than willing to throw my leg over mean, angry broncs for a ride that could end my life without any fear, but was not willing to approach Sandy for what was—in my mind—fear of rejection and loss. How does that make any sense at all?

I remember telling my brother Billy about Sandy and how much I wanted to talk to her but was afraid. Billy told me to talk to her and let her know I was interested in getting to know her. I told him I was not anyone she would want to know. He said I was probably right 'cause I had already defeated myself in getting to know the girl. It would be just like saying 'I can't ride that horse' before I even tried and finding out I was right because I was negative about it. Billy always had good advice for his little brother.

As a boy, I took things at face value and did not question what I saw or what I thought I saw. In reality, Sandy was a one-eyed jack to me. I could only see the beauty that I beheld. I did not know about her personality. I did not know if she was a nice person or even a girl I would want to know. We lived and moved in different worlds with different people. My world would not make room for Sandy, and I am very certain her world had no space for me. For me to see the other side of this girl would take more work than I was willing to give. So I did nothing about it.

I got good at bronc riding and gained tremendous self-confidence in my ability to defy death, but never got up the nerve to speak to Sandy. Lost opportunities are all part of growing up in this world. Some losses lead us to places we never wanted to go, and some save us from what we never needed anyway. Looking back over that time in my life, I would not change very many things if any at all. Sandy has no idea of the loss I thought I suffered by not getting to know her, and she never will. My perception of loss has changed many times over the years. I have found that what once was the real deal for me has never stayed the same for very long.

In the fall of 1963, I attended the Brawley, California Cattle Call Rodeo as an entrant in Little Britches Senior Bronc Riding and won a very nice buckle for my efforts. I add this to this story only because of the horse I drew to score high in the event. The horse was a very active, high-bucking, side-twisting mare named Sandy Girl. Seemed ironic to me at the time that I would get the nod to win the event in my age bracket on a horse named after my heart throb back at school. No one ever knew about it except Billy and he just laughed.

After high school, I joined the US Navy and shipped out to see the world. After basic training and flight school, I became a member of Crew 7 in VP-28, flying over the Pacific and wondering how Sandy was doing. The only real memory I took with me from high school was the thought that one day I would return to Yuma, find Sandy, and tell her of my desire to get to know her. Sandy went on to become Miss Arizona with all of the fame that brings to a young woman. I did not follow her career after learning about her becoming Miss Arizona. I was too busy with my own life to concern myself with hers. When I think about my time in high school, I still think about that girl I knew named Sandy.

The years since high school have been up and down with a lot of pain and a lot of joy. My life is now total bliss and those old memories are foreign but still comfortable. Sure hope Sandy has fared as well in her life. Funny to think of how the things that we did and what we didn't do bring us to where we are today. It's now 54 years since I last saw Sandy, the girl of my once-upon-a-time dreams. You can bet dreams certainly do change. Frustration and guilt are part of the way I feel about that time in my life. But along with that is also a very calm feeling that it doesn't really matter.

If I was destined to do something other than what I did, I believe I would have done it. Chance, happenstance, or predisposition, it's all the same in my mind. We are who we are because of the choices we make and have made in our lives. To look back after all these years is pointless if we are trying to find answers as to why we did what we did or did not do.

Perhaps my writing about those times is my way of finding the truth. I do believe the truth will set us free. Free from ignorance I'm sure and free from want of a better life. I have all the joy I could ever find in this life and I have tried to share it with others.

Nice to have a memory of a girl that is warm and comfortable to go along with memories of hard leather and unforgiving rodeo arena grounds. Sandy is as fresh in my mind today as she ever was. I'd like to thank her for the memories; I don't know how except to write about it. A boy growing into a man in Yuma needed a pin-up girl and Sandy was mine. Congratulations on becoming Miss Arizona. You will always be Miss KOFA High School to me, my teenage queen.

ProLog:

Tucson

"I know you, you're that boy from school." That's how it started with me and her over the internet. Two people out of the blue not really looking for a connection with someone they used to know many years before. Here in 2022 looking back to 1964, seemed like a dream, 58 years later. A photo in the mind's eye coupled with a few written words does not make a very clear picture of a person from the past. Both widowers since 2020, what we want and what is real are often so different it will take our breath away. In this case, reality was starting to become true, that what we wanted was just a simple connection and recognition of who we were to one another.

It has been said before when the legend becomes reality print the legend.

I finally met this woman and got to see and hear her for the first time in my life. We went on an adventure in Tucson her home town and I feel great about getting to know a small part of her and her world. As it turns out she is a very closed-off and private person. She was gracious to me and showed me the parts of her life that I would never have known had we not hooked up on the internet. We connected with each other on many levels and it's hard to mention each one.

After spending time with her I found that we are really very different, in our personal values and the way we see the world around us. I have found in this life that differences can attract or repel as each person's convictions lead them. In the time we had together, we realized how different we are and how we are from worlds entirely separate and apart. It was good to meet in this time of life we had together. On separate paths, as we are, we found no common ground with which to pursue a relationship other than renewing old times of our past lives.

A fitting ending to the story about the girl from so long ago. I will always love the memories I have of the times in my youth with a girl I never really knew. My life in this instance has come full circle and I finally realize that the girl I did not know in High School, is the same girl I did not get to know in Tucson. 58 years of love for a person that is underserving of my affection or time. I'm fine with the legend of Sandy Girl as I knew it and wrote it.

Ω

Riding My Dreams

The 39 Brand

As I walked up to the pen that they were in, I could see that some were resting and some were moving around restlessly. Waiting around for the show was something they had done many times before no doubt and some were a bit anxious about it. I stood and watched them for a while but I could not tell which ones were mean or angry. These were rodeo horses used for saddle bronc and bareback riding, and before the show began for the day I was there to see them. I wondered which one I would draw for a chance at a successful ride. No matter which one I got to ride first, I hoped it would be my day to shine as a participant.

Only one of them paid any attention to me. As far as I could tell, the horse that looked at me did so with a bit of interest and came up to me. Sniffed around me for a moment or two as I held out my hand in a gesture of friendship and told him who I was. His eyes were clear and he looked at me with concern about why I was there that morning. He took note of the rig I held in my grip for saddle bronc riding and he seemed to know I was there to ride. He sniffed around my back pocket where I had shoved my gloves covered with pine tar.

Everything about me was of interest to him. I could tell my being there didn't bother him. Then in an instant, he was gone to the far side of the pen, and then back again to stand in front of me. He was a paint horse and really stood out with all the bays and other dun-colored horses. None of the others even acknowledged I was there. Just a skinny youngster standing outside their pen looking in.

I don't know how long I stood there with this new friend I had made, but soon I had to go and get checked in and draw the number to pin on my back. Wasn't a lot of competition at this rodeo, maybe five other guys, and I didn't know any of them.

Later that day I got my draw and it turned out to be the paint horse from the pen. I knew who he was, but did he know me from earlier? We often tend to dismiss the memory skills of animals we meet in life. I, for one, would say we are wrong about them. They remember things that even we forget.

Wondering about my ride on that paint horse? Did very well and scored high, but not high enough to take top honors that day. It wasn't the horse's fault that I didn't do all that well. He posted a good score, but I just wasn't that animated during the ride. I guess I was too comfortable in what I was doing to make it look like I was really working it.

After that first, go 'round of riding, I stopped by the pen of the bucking stock and looked for that paint horse. He was there and came up to me again as if to say, "There you are. How'd we do?" I thanked him for the ride and said I'd be proud to ride him again if I got the chance. I had an apple in my pack that I brought from home for lunch and he was happy to take it from me. He appeared to almost smile at me about the gift I gave him. As I walked away, he followed me down the fence line of the pen.

When I came back the next day and looked in the pen to find him, he wasn't there. Never did know his name; only thing about him that I remember was a big 39 brand on his left hip, his high kicks, and his gentleness with me as a stranger. Didn't bother me much that he was gone 'cause that second day I did well on another horse and took home a buckle. Wasn't a great buckle that I won, just something to say I did good at that event. My entry fee for the event would have bought me a better buckle at the western wear store in Yuma.

The second day was special for another reason. The rodeo was held just 10 miles south of my home in Yuma, and Mom and Dad were there to see me ride, as well as to watch Billy and Duke do their thing in the timed steer roping event. They even brought Grandpa with them as he wanted to see his grandson stay on a rank horse for at least eight seconds. It was special to me 'cause Mom had never seen me ride before. Made me do real good so as to please her.

Mom and Dad said they had a good time watching their boy ride. I found it comforting to have my own cheering section. Cheering that I wouldn't get hurt anyway. Mom said I looked so small on that horse and she wished I'd find another hobby that wasn't so dangerous. Dad said I was doing just fine and that I was coming into being the rider I was meant to be. Grandpa said he had not been to a rodeo in well on to 30 years or so. Said it was a lot of fun and it was great to see me ride. My brother Billy did well in the roping that day, and his combined scores put him on top.

After the rodeo was over we all had tamales and fun at the town gathering. Billy got Mom up on Duke and she took a spin around on him for a time; Dad did also. Grandpa said 'No, thank you,' as his riding days were long gone. Billy offered Duke a tamale but he didn't want it and we all laughed. Time to spend with family. It never gets better than that, I'll tell you.

Some things in life can't be reasoned away easily. When I became a police officer a full decade later in my search for a career, I was given the badge number 39. Didn't think much about that number at the time but for some reason, I do now. I wore that badge as a brand for eight years of my life and tried to stay as true to it as that paint horse with the 39 brand on his hip was to me. Had a lot of high kicks in that eight-year span but came out of it on my feet.

I don't know why I remember these events after all this time. I think about the days of my youth and the things that I did. The places I went and the people and horses that I met along the way. I remember the horses more than the people I met and dealt with. Might just be the way I was brought up and what I thought was important. Could be that the horses were more real to me and more honest in the way they presented themselves.

I remember my father telling me people will always appear as one-eyed jacks and you have to work at seeing their other side to know the whole person. Horses don't lie and they don't put on a false front. Horses don't hide anything from you. How you treat them is how they respond to you. What you see is what you get. I've been bitten, stepped on, thrown, smashed in a pen, and downright beaten up by horses, but they've never really shown anger at me as a person, just me as a rider, as they did their job as trained.

Fear that what I was doing while riding was going to hurt me was never a part of my thinking. I didn't fear the unknown, and yes, it did hurt me sometimes. But that was all part of learning how not to do the thing I was trying to do. I wanted to be mean and tough while doing my riding in the arena. I knew the horses were trained to be aggressive and to act wild for the crowd and the judges. The more they bucked the better the score for them and for me. It was all about learning how to be good at it.

Learning has not occurred until behavior changes. I learned that early on in my time in rodeo. Sometimes I could see the hurt coming my way; other times it happened without warning from out of the blue. Hanging up in the chute, rolling into the fence, a horse falling down with me on him—it was all part of the sport of bronc riding. You had to take the bad to get the good. To my way of thinking, it was worth all the pain and hurt to get good at something others wouldn't even try. Shooting for the moon was not how I thought about it at the time. It was just an honest effort.

During my teen years, it was always about horses and what I could accomplish with them. School held no interest for me at that time. Being with my big brother was all I knew and my aim was trying to be a grownup just like him. Through it all, my family gave me the freedom and encouragement to choose what I did with my time as a boy in Yuma. I will always be grateful for that.

Throughout our lifetime people come and go. Some are good and some are bad. Forgetting the bad, enjoying the good, and moving on is the best we can do. But horses--regardless of how they act--remain in your heart and mind forever. Getting thrown is all part of life, whether in a rodeo arena, in your career, or in your love life. Because of the horses in my life, I remember the other parts. If not for them I wouldn't be able to recall those times. I remember because the horses, my brother, and Mom and Dad were there with me.

Ω

Patch

So vivid is my memory about the time I spent with the horses at Don's place in Yuma. One horse comes to mind during those formative years of learning about these creatures. Don had a black stallion named Patch. Patch was said to be mean-spirited and not safe to be around for anyone. I learned that what people say is not always the way it is—especially when it comes to horses. I found Patch to be a gentle, loving animal who just wanted some attention from those around him. I tried to always have a carrot or an apple for him. Every time I came to him with a treat of any kind he would raise his left front hoof off the ground as if to say 'thank you'.

I spent a summer getting to know Patch and the other horses I was helping to care for. Patch was very high-spirited indeed, but in no way did he ever show his mean side to me. He had a black coat that glistened an iridescent blue in the sunlight, and he had a white blaze on his forehead in the shape of an elongated star. Patch always wore a black headstall with his name stitched on the side in silver. His mane and tail were more of a dark blonde than any other color and he looked regal in every way. When he ran he moved with grace and always held his head high and his tail up. To me, he was majestic and handsome beyond measure.

There was also a mare at Don's named Zona--which I guessed was short for Arizona. She was a golden blonde color and very gentle with a boy that was new to horses. Patch and Zona had already gotten together and she was pregnant when I first met her. A few months later Zona gave birth to her fourth offspring. I was there to witness the event in its entirety. Yes sir, God showed me the magic of life as it begins right there in the hay of a horse stall in Yuma.

Can't say that witnessing this event made me love Zona any more than I already did, but I felt like a proud papa being there to see her give birth. Patch seemed very proud to have played a large part in the arrival of the newest member of the horse community at Don's place. The foal, a male, was perfect in every way. He was a blood-red and white paint horse with four white stocking hoofs attached to his unsteady, non-working legs. The little guy was absolutely gorgeous.

It took him a while but he finally got to where he could stand on those new legs and found his mother's milk. I was amazed to learn that he did not know where his momma's teat was, but once he found it he was a natural at sucking. Don had already dipped the umbilical cord stub with iodine-- something else for me to learn. Being there at the ranch was the best part of life for me. Could not believe I was actually included in that way of life. I felt sure I would always be a part of that horse family that I had adopted as my own. Don said he named the new little guy Mix because of his color and because Don always revered movie star Tom Mix.

In the time I got to know Mix, I felt a real attachment to him because I had witnessed his entry into this world. Zona knew me and she had no problem with me being around her and her new foal. She did, however, have a problem with Patch wanting to be near her and the little guy. That, in turn, caused Billy's horse Duke to be agitated, and soon the other horses all had a problem with each other. Having a new foal was not all fun and games; it caused a lot of work for everyone. One thing was sure: Zona and Mix were not going anywhere soon.

Some weeks later I had to come to grips with another part of life in the horse business. It broke my heart when Don, the owner of the string of horses, up and sold Patch. I was told it was strictly business and nothing personal. Wasn't business to me--it was definitely personal.

Moving ahead six years from that time, I found myself in full rodeo mode going from place to place trying my hand at saddle bronc riding. On one particular day, we were in Wellton, Arizona, a small farming and ranching community about 30 miles east of Yuma, for a roping event with Billy, my older brother. It was being held at the McElhaney Cattle Company Roping Arena and there was money offered for best round by anyone who entered. Billy was a very gifted roper and always had his hand in events in and around the state. I was there to watch and learn as always, and to lend a helping hand as needed for Billy and Duke.

Billy told me to keep my eye on a black horse and its rider as they were very good and his most stiff competition. He said the roper's name was Rick and that he lived in Wellton.

As the day went on I saw a lot of great roping and a lot of beginners trying to be ropers. Billy was intent on doing well and there was a good bit of money on the line for top hand. Some people had driven from a long way off to be at this gathering. Sure were a lot of people trying their hand at the event.

I noticed a horse in the roping event that had a striking resemblance to Patch--the horse at Don's from so many years earlier. The size was right, the coloring of his blue/black coat shining in the sun was the same. Even the mane and tail being a dark blonde were identical to Patch, as was the elongated star on his forehead. I had to find out about this horse and I assumed the rider was this Rick fellow that Billy had mentioned.

Since there were a lot of people competing in this timed event, there was plenty of time between rounds for me to ask Rick about his horse. He said he bought the horse some years before at an auction over in Brawley, California, and he was very happy with the way the horse took to roping. He called his horse by another name and said he didn't know anything about his past other than Brawley. I mentioned Yuma and a guy named Don who owned a similar horse about six years earlier. Rick said he had no knowledge of any of that for this horse. When I mentioned the name Patch, Rick said, "Hold on a minute" and he went over to his truck.

Billy had walked up about then, and we both waited to see what this Rick guy had. When he returned he held up an old black headstall with the word 'Patch' stitched into the side in silver. He said it came with a bunch of gear he picked up with the horse at the auction in Brawley. He said he never used it 'cause it was older and he didn't know it belonged to his horse. I took it to mean this could be Patch, and I wondered if the horse would remember me. I asked Rick if he ever saw his horse raise his left front hoof off the ground when he got fed. He said he hadn't.

I walked up to Rick's horse and stood in front of him so he could see me clearly. He raised his head and shook it as if to say he did know me. He moved closer to me and smacked his lips as if asking for a carrot or a treat. I had always done that to make friends with him back in those earlier days. I stroked his neck and rubbed his muzzle in recognition of who he was and told him it was me after all these years.

When I called out his name "Patch," his ears became alert and he raised his head and whinnied. He then lifted his left front hoof off the ground as if to say "I remember you. Where's my treat?" I was sure it was Patch and told Rick about our times together in Yuma. I told him about the foal named Mix out of Zona and how I was there to see life begin for Patch's little boy.

Billy knew Rick from several contests around the countryside and Rick knew of Billy and Duke and had seen them at a lot of events. While they talked I took time to be with Patch one last time before the day came to a close. Patch and I walked around the pens and roping lot. I did not have to hold on to his lead at all. He followed me all over the place.

That chance meeting was profound to me. I was meant to see Patch again and actually say goodbye the way I wanted to all those years ago. I offered to buy the headstall from Rick. He said with a story like mine I should have the thing, and he gave it to me. I still have that old piece of leather and buckles with the stitching on the side spelling out Patch. I never saw Patch again at any of the events we went to around Yuma. Often thought of trying to find him out in Wellton, but he wasn't my horse. He belonged to someone else and that was the end of that friendship.

I am convinced that horses have a lengthy and vivid memory of people and places. I was beyond happy to see Patch again and even happier that Patch truly did remember me. It was a heartfelt meeting and a sad goodbye all rolled into one. Patch had a good home with a caring owner that loved him and wanted the best for him, just like I did. After all, is said and done, we are all seeking a loving companion and a good home. With tear-filled eyes, I said Goodbye to Patch for the last time.

Ω

Jill and Ringer

I recall one particular Christmas day during my youth, Mom was feeling poorly and stayed in bed for most of the day. Dad was a fireman and had to work. My brother Billy was off with a girl who he thought would soon be his wife. And I was left alone to do what I did when I was in charge of my day.

I had to go feed Duke and care for the other horses down at Don's as I always did. I rode my bicycle down to the pens and started in on my chores. After finishing-up brushing and feeding Duke and Zona and doing my job of mucking out the stalls, I noticed one of the mares that Don was boarding was down in the far pasture and not moving. I went to investigate and found she was not conscious. I couldn't get her to respond at all. The horse's owner was a girl that came to care for her every day. I had her phone number in a book in Don's tack room so I called her and told her about her horse. It wasn't long 'til she showed up and we both went to see about the horse in the pasture. Soon the vet showed up and it began to look bad for the horse that was down.

"Wait a minute. You're saying that you don't know why my healthy, normal horse won't get up and you want me to spend a bunch of money running tests that also may tell us nothing? And you can try a couple of treatments but if they don't work then I will have to put her to sleep? She was fine yesterday!"

The vet explained the cost of intensive care for horses in slings and often the owner finds that there is no way they can afford that. This leaves the owner in a very difficult position where they don't feel comfortable putting their horse to sleep without giving her a chance, but they don't want her to suffer. They feel guilty for giving up on the horse and just don't understand what could have happened to cause this situation. The horse's temperature was elevated and the vet said his best guess was colic.

I didn't understand the medical implications of a horse being down, but it became clear that getting her up and standing was the key to her survival. If we could not do that then she would stay there till she did get up or the decision was made to put her to sleep.

The vet had a slide rigged up in no time and with large nylon straps the downed horse was pulled back to the shelter of the stall area and covered with blankets. Seemed that the agitation in her resting position made her try real hard to stand, and with our help, she did stand up. Wobbly on her legs, but standing nonetheless. The vet checked her for blockage in her intestines and found nothing but gave her a warm enema just the same and forced some pills down her throat along with a good helping of water.

After about an hour she seemed to be more steady on her legs and was walking around a lot better. The girl said she would be with her horse till the situation improved so I left her with my home phone number and went on home. I didn't think she would call me for anything, but I guessed it was the thing to do at the time.

The girl's name was Jill and she was a prospective rodeo queen and barrel racer in the area. She was pretty and I guessed that she was about 18 years old. Going through a situation like that makes for a bond with people, and I did that with Jill. Jill told me of her dreams to be the best she could be in barrel racing and one day be a singing star as well as a star in movies. I guess if you're going to dream then you might as well dream big. The horse's name was Ringer and she was a beauty just like her owner.

The vet came often and took special care of Ringer and it was not long before Ringer was behaving like nothing had ever happened. She was a very sweet horse to me and I liked being around her. Jill and I agreed to Ringer's care and grooming. I was hired to care for Ringer when I was at the place and to call Jill if anything was going on. She paid me a small amount each week. I looked at it as money coming in for doing what I was going to do anyway. When Jill spoke to me she always confided in me that one day she dreamed of owning a large horse property and having plenty of money to operate it.

Billy took an interest in the goings-on with Jill and Ringer and watched her practice. It was only natural that he should watch her practice and she should watch him practice. Kind of a mutual admiration society formed with us.

As it turned out Jill didn't have any way to haul her horse to events around the area and Billy did. So at my insistence, they started hauling their horses in the two-up horse trailer that Billy had. I didn't think for one minute that a romance would begin with Jill and Billy but it did, and I was like the third spoon in the fudge sundae. Got to where three in the cab of Billy's truck was a crowd. The old truck was a 1949 International and had a small cab, to say the least.

Being 14 going on 30 and watching this lovey-dovey business wasn't what I had in mind with my brother. But love knows no bounds and will grow where it is least expected. As the little brother, I was still part of the threesome and had not been discarded as a nuisance. Next thing you know, Billy was bringing Jill over to the house to meet Mom and Dad. Bringing Jill to dinner at the house was commonplace and the duo were inseparable. I still had worth and they kept me around to help out with the horses.

Time marches on and things happen that even the most casual of observers can see plainly in front of their noses. Jill indeed became involved in the Silver Spur Rodeo Queen Pageant in Yuma. Her fame, beauty, and riding skills took the hometown girl to new heights of recognition for her barrel racing. She went on to become a Miss Arizona Rodeo Queen in about 1968 and runner-up for Miss Arizona. Billy told me Jill made it to the PRC National Finals Rodeo and won top honors for her efforts in Barrel Racing. I did not know Jill could sing, but sing she did and made her debut as the next rising country singing star in Nashville. Next for her was Hollywood and all that it can do for a girl that is willing to excel in that world and that kind of work. Jill, for all intents and purposes, was gone from little ol' Yuma. Gone from little ol' Billy and me, and gone from the tiny world of riding Ringer in small-town rodeos. Billy and Jill kept in touch over the years and he would tell me about her from time to time. For me, she was out of sight and out of mind.

Jill changed her name for whatever the reasons are; that people like her change their names. She became a sensation in her new endeavors and never looked back on tiny little Yuma. Even if she did look back, we never noticed it. Billy was happy for her and said what he always said about hurt to any degree at all: "Just put dirt on it and don't tell Mom."

As far as I know, Jill is still the star she always wanted to be. Living in Nashville, married to a music producer, and living on a large horse ranch just as she dreamed it. I corresponded with her by email some years ago, and she did remember me and Billy fondly and thanked me for being a huge part of her life way back then. She wrote about her days riding for glory and fame on Ringer and how her time in Yuma was still held as precious memories for her. I didn't comprehend how much older she was than I was at the time in Yuma. But in due time my interest in girls did come around and I have often thought about Jill and the times we were together.

A couple of dozen years later Billy and I talked about Jill, Ringer and the times we knew back in those Yuma days. It seemed like a make-believe world to both of us and in the big scheme of things in this world, it was like a fantasy and never had a moment of truth or reality. According to Billy, it was like a great big, wonderful, and expensive cigar that gets lit and burns for a time bringing joy to the smoker, and then, as all cigars do, burns out and gets discarded. Odd for Billy to compare his love interest to be like a cigar, but then we all deal with love and loss differently. I guess his way was as good as any.

Now at my age in life, I can look back just like anyone can and visualize those days the way I want to. I never felt huge in anyone's life except my own and even at that I was only a pebble in a boot compared to others. Memories are all we have in the end. Memories are good to have especially the ones that live in us fondly.

Ω

Billy and Duke

I had childhood heroes as all kids do from time to time. Roy Rogers, Gene Autry, Rex Allen, and Hop-along Cassidy, just to name a few. I went to see them at the movie theater as a boy growing up in my hometown. Six guns, saddles, horses, and, of course, riding and shooting were the big thing. As I got a bit older, around 10 or 11 years old, I found a real-life hero in my brother Billy. He was bigger, better, and real in every sense of the word. To say he was my hero is an understatement. He was my big brother and my pal.

Billy was a roper and competed in timed events at rodeos. At 16 years old, he was good at it and he loved doing it. To me, he was the best there ever was at the sport. Billy got me started in rodeo sports and encouraged me in every way. I started out mutton busting and then steer riding. I could not believe how much fun it was to crash into the dirt and then get up to do it again.

Billy was five years older than me, and he was more than just a big brother for me to look up to. Billy gave me the opportunity to learn new things and to grow as a boy in a man's world. I learned how to get up when I was down and how to try again when I failed. Through all the bumps and bruises I found a new way of dealing with life. I learned that no matter what happens to us, as we try our best to be our best, it only matters that we try and never stop trying.

Billy had a horse named Duke who was part Morgan and part everything else, I guess. Duke was a chestnut-colored horse with a fiery red mane and tail. He was chosen to be a roping horse because of his legs, according to Billy. He said Duke would grow into them over time. Billy always referred to Duke as a rig. I found out what that meant some years later and of course, it was a curiosity to me. At three years old, Duke had learned his job as a roping horse and Billy worked with him almost every day.

Duke was four years old when I came into the rodeo world and he was exceptionally good at his job by then. He had a shorter stride and used his rear well, according to Billy, and got him to the calf quickly for the catch. Billy said he came out of the chute with a flat gait and kept steady as he went. All of this I heard, but it meant little to me as I was not a roper. I asked him once

51

if Dad ever came to see him rope and he said he did, just not often. I guessed by that answer that Dad would come to see me as well whenever his work would allow.

Billy had won many an event all around our hometown and at sanctioned rodeos. And he had won a drawer full of buckles. Billy always said the more you try to win the more chances are that you will win. When you get hurt just rub dirt on it, and above all else don't tell Mom about it. Took me a while to realize that Mom had nothing to do with what Billy was telling me. He was saying that hurt and losing are not things to tell anyone about, just save the telling for the wins. I decided not to tell Mom even if I did win. If I told anyone about my failures and wins it was Dad. He was on my side in this activity that I had taken a liking to but wasn't real vocal about his support.

I was 14 when I really got going in Little Britches events. I purely did love saddle bronc riding and I was sure I was getting better at it by not falling down as much. During that time Dad told me that sometimes life gives us a bigger shovel than we can use fully loaded. That's when we need to back off the load on the shovel to what we can handle. It was his way of saying that I needed to slow down and not push so hard and it would come.

Growing up in Yuma I was well aware of how hot it gets. Didn't matter to me and Billy, we were going to do this rodeo thing no matter what the weather did. Rained on us something fierce up in Prescott, but we did not slow down on account of that. Duke was as sure-footed in the mud as he was on hard pack back home. It seemed like the sky was the limit for us boys and riding and roping was to be our calling in life. But everything in this life has a time for doing and a time for quitting. There are always others that help us in those decisions. Not all of them are human.

Changes in life come to all of us in time. Billy got himself married and had a baby boy, Robert. At 22, Billy decided to hang up his ropes. Duke helped him to make that decision. He had said many times if he or Duke got hurt, that would be the end of his roping.

It was at a roping event in Casa Grande and a lot of money was on the line for the winner. Duke was acting a bit strange to Billy but nothing that would take him out of the competition. Billy had a great first round and it was looking really good for him. Then came the time for it all to change. Duke came out exceptionally fast, and for whatever reason went down and went down hard. Billy got twisted up and spit out in a heap on the ground and it took him several minutes to regain his feet. I was, of course, off the fence and headed for Billy as fast as I could run. What I planned to do when I got there was not yet in my head. Billy was visibly shaken by the fall but still had the presence of mind to look after Duke.

Duke was still down when I got to Billy. It took a good deal of time to get Duke up and he was not in good shape at all. Of course, that was the end of that day's event for us. Billy was hurt pretty bad and in a lot of pain.

We left Duke in the corral there at the roping grounds and took Billy to the hospital. Glad I came with Billy 'cause I was the one who drove the pickup truck even without a driver's license. Billy had suffered a dislocated shoulder, two cracked ribs, and a badly bruised knee. Needless to say, he was not a happy boy. Duke was able to load up in the trailer with the help of friends at the event and seemed to be all right standing. I was worried about both of them more than anyone. It was all I could do to get Billy in the truck and comfortable for the ride home. The people at the roping event said, "Thanks for coming boys, better luck next time." No money for the day seemed to bother Billy the most.

Back home the vet took a good deal of time to decide what had happened and said Duke suffered a hind suspensory ligament tear that was high up and hard to treat. Outlook for recovery would be about 12 months, maybe longer. No such injury ever healed to the point that the horse would be back to normal, and a year down the road was a lifetime for Billy.

A man who Billy knew approached him and said he would like to buy Duke. He said he had watched the horse develop over the years and knew what he was worth as a roping horse. He also knew of the injury and the time it would take to get him back in shape. He was willing to take all that on for a selling price if Billy would agree. Billy told the man that the horse was his partner and that he loved that horse. Then Billy took me aside and said, "Horses are a business and they are a partner in this business. You can't live your life in the shadow of a business partner."

The man restated his offer, the deal was made, and Duke went to his new home. Apparently, the fact that Duke still retained his testicles (Remember him being a rig?) for breeding purposes was the main factor in the sale. I was still not ready for this end of the horse business. Twice in my life people had sold horses right out from under me and they were not even my horses. Where do you get the mentality and the heart to sell your life's work and walk away from it? I needed to toughen up my heart if I was going to survive in this life. Took several years for me to get over this separation of heart and business.

To this day I don't think I ever sat on Duke for any reason at all. Duke was Billy's horse and no one else ever rode him. Broke my heart when Billy sold him and it took me a long time to get over the hurt. I know it hurt Billy too, but he never showed it. Years later I found out that Billy had hurt himself in the wreck with Duke much more than he ever let on.

Billy was a journeyman printer by trade and moved to San Diego during the time I was away in the Navy. While in San Diego, Billy owned his own printing business and eventually purchased the building it was in. He had ups and downs in his personal life but then, as I have said many times, Billy was not a quitter. He never talked about his time spent roping or Duke. It was in his past and best left there. I will say without hesitation that Billy and Duke were an unqualified success.

Many years later I talked to Billy about his rodeo days, and he said it was a necessary part of his life and the most fun he had ever had. He said he had no regrets about any part of it. Billy told me the proudest he had been during those days was when I started getting the hang of riding. He took particular pleasure in telling me it was his instruction and devotion to my learning that got me through it all. He also pointed out that Mom was not at all happy about his role in my activities. Mom had begged him to watch over me closely and not to let anything happen to me. I loved the man Billy was and I loved the man he became. I would sure like to think I learned something by watching him and being around him all those many years ago. I can't help but believe I did.

Billy passed away in 2011. If our dreams of the afterlife are true, he's roping again on Duke in the big arena in the sky. I never had to search for a real live hero in my life. I had my big brother Billy.

Last One to Ride

Seems silly to me now to recount my young days around horses. I was not raised on a farm or a ranch. I was never a cowboy or a horseman. I never owned a horse, and I never wanted to own a horse. The time I spent with and around horses was about learning to care for them and to know them as the animals they are. For some unexplainable reason, my love for horses and my disappointment about the way some people treat them led me into the sport of saddle bronc riding. I had to prove to myself I could be around horses and not have to care for them as pets. Horses became my way of gaining self-respect and learning to fit into the man's world that I had come to know.

Riding rough stock that are encouraged to buck was a novel way of spending my time. Sports in school held no interest for me. Being with my older brother, Billy, was what I wanted to do. Billy got me started in trying my hand at riding horses in rodeos. It was a thrill and challenging for a youngster who was new to the sport.

First I had to find a good rig (saddle) to use. Billy knew a man that had a couple of them. He no longer did rodeo so we went to see him. Had to learn how to use it and set it up for my legs to fit the stirrups just right.

I had to make my boots a bit larger than my foot so they would come off if I got hung up in a stirrup, which I did several times. Asked Billy how to do that since a new pair of boots was not possible with my meager earnings. "You could wear a couple pair of thicker socks to get it done and leather would stretch, or you could do it the easy way." He said to just fill a plastic bag part way with water and stuff it in the boot with a couple of rags behind it to keep it in there, and then stick them in the freezer for a day. I tried it and it worked.

I had to find some short shank spurs to wear and learn to tie them on the right way. Billy said short shank spurs would not get hung up in the rein or my rigging so easily. With them, my feet would move more freely and give the judges a good view of my raking motion as I rode.

Had to have a braided rein to use which was all part of this game. Learning how to hold the rein, how to give just enough slack, and knowing each horse was not the same was always a challenge. Pretty sure I broke the little finger on my right hand about a dozen times. The stockmen and other riders were always willing to help out with advice.

The one thing I didn't have to start out with were chaps to wear, and many is the time I wished I had purchased a pair and wore them right from the start. Once I got a pair they sure did help me stay in touch with the swells of the rigging. I often asked Billy how he knew so much and he would say "Been there, done that." Then it got harder as I became aware of the hardness of the ground and the fact that I had very little if any control over how I fell. Trying not to fall was the goal and it was getting better as I went.

Practicing seemed to be the key to getting better. Billy said the more you ride the more you learn. Sometimes I wish he had told the horses that I was good enough and they didn't have to make me look bad in front of a whole bunch of people. Getting hung up in the chute, having a bucking strap slap me upside the head, and having my rein come undone all became part of the game. No one told me the horses fall down, too. They get hung up in the chute and in the gate, they turn the wrong way from what I think they will turn, they even climb the fence in the arena.

Hurting back, hurting hip, out-of-joint shoulder, bangs, and bruises became my world in this thing I absolutely loved to do. Figured a broken bone would be my bad luck in this thing or the loss of an eye or a tooth, but it never happened. I'm very certain that if I had continued I was overdue for something like that to occur. Didn't have the protective vests and helmets with face masks like the riders do today. Ruined many a hat trying to look the part of a genuine cowboy for a whole bunch of people I did not know.

Once at the Somerton, Arizona rodeo I had drawn a very good horse to ride in the event and was waiting my turn. Then suddenly some other cowboy was out riding the horse I was supposed to ride. The judges scored him very well for his effort and then realized I was not the rider on the horse as drawn. The stock people had loaded my horse in his assigned chute, and his drawn horse in the chute for me to ride. So they disqualified both of us from the competition. I didn't even get to ride his draw in the event. Politics does play into the sport and mistakes do occur. That was not a good day for me. Bad days are all part of doing what can be done but just doesn't get done. Not today anyway.

Up in Prescott, Arizona at the 4th of July Rodeo which I had to skip school for, it was raining and didn't seem like it would be letting up anytime soon. Out of the chute I went, and the horse lost his footing and went down in the mud. I was still hanging on as he stumbled to his feet and off we went and down we went. The third time he got up he was not interested in doing his thing, so I stepped off. I had made it to the buzzer with this horse but we sure weren't doing real good at bucking. The judges were being kind to me on that occasion and since I and the horse put on a good show they scored me well. I was looking for another ride after that as re-rides are generally given for faults by the horse, but settled for my best score. After my other rides, I had a great aggregate score and went out on top. Seems no other rider had spurred out of the chute and all were disqualified except for me. Mud was what I had to wear home with a sore body and a very beautiful buckle. It all seemed like a dream to me. The horse I rode in the rain--or at least tried to-- that kept falling down was named Dancer. We surely did dance for those people to get a score.

The event lasted four days for me, two of which were school days, but then I didn't give a rip about school. Long drive home to Yuma on a Sunday night to get back for school on Monday. Didn't really want to go back to school. I was hurting and sore all over. Billy had to go back to work, but he didn't mind 'cause he loved his printing job and always said it would be his future, not rodeo.

There was a lady taking photographs there in Prescott, and she took several shots of me in and out of the arena. Wasn't till some 50-plus years later that I found out the lady photographer, Mary Dove, had made a painting out of one of my photos. She called it "Six Men and a Horse" and it is hanging in her gallery in Sedona with a hefty price tag on it. I feel right proud of that and told her so by email. I am not immortal but get the feeling someone somewhere is enjoying my efforts more than I ever did.

One spring we drove up to a rodeo in Wickenburg, Arizona. For a spring day, it was hot and miserable. Reckon the horse I had drawn felt out of sorts because of all the dust and the heat, 'cause he was not going to settle down in the chute. I tried several times to get on him but he kept throwing a fit and climbing up out of the chute. I could ease down on him but I could not get my feet to stay in the stirrups.

After trying several times to mount the horse, one of the chute workers asked me what I was going to do. I said very plainly, "I plan to ride this miserable son-of-a-bitch as soon as I can get both feet in a stirrup to stay. Hell, I'd settle for both feet in the same stirrup."

The man said, "Watch yer language here, son. This is a Christian event." I said I was sorry. He told me to stick my feet in the stirrups first and then drop down on him and he would jerk the gate open as fast as he could. He told me that wearing a hat was normal for riding in this rodeo. I told him I would be proud to wear one but "mine is down underneath this son-of-a-bitch somewhere and I ain't gonna reach down to get it." Once again the man scolded me for my language. Billy was there and offered me his hat.

I took the good advice about the stirrups so I did just that, and he was indeed fast on the chute gate. As he pulled the gate open he yelled "All right, boys, let this son-of-a-bitch out." The ride was spectacular and the horse was as good a bucking bronc as I have ever scored with. Billy said it was as good a ride as he had ever seen me make and a good deal better than most. If Billy was pleased with my efforts then I was pleased.

Went to Nogales, Arizona for a gathering of ropers and riders. I don't think they called it a sanctioned rodeo but just a get-together. Billy went because there was money in it for him if he won. He did win and it was a very nice total for his efforts.

I got into the riding part of the event and didn't do so good. Maybe it was the long drive to get there, maybe it was the burrito I ate before the event, or maybe it just wasn't my day. At any rate, this young girl seemed to be infatuated with me and was all over me after I failed to ride well. She was hugging and kissing me and generally making a nuisance of herself over me. Billy told me "I said you would be liked by the girls." I got away from that girl and we left for home. Billy laughed all the way to Gila Bend over the deal and we still had 118 more miles to go. I never even knew her name.

In the fall of each year, we headed to Brawley, California for their Cattle Call Rodeo which was always a great event. A bit further than the drive to El Centro, California, it was about 78 miles from Billy's place in Yuma. I won a buckle there and thought so much of it I gave it to my dad for safekeeping. It meant a lot to him. Mom gave it back to me after he passed away. I loved the fact that Dad enjoyed the buckle even more than I enjoyed winning it.

At one event we attended--might have been Prescott, Arizona--I tore my left boot darn near in half on a chute gate. The boots were alligator lizard and I really did like them, but torn as they were, they were no good to me.

I took the boots down to see Grandpa in Yuma, and he said he thought he could fix the torn boot without too much trouble since the sole was still intact.

First, he stuffed the boot with wet ironwood bark and then proceeded to glue it back together using mesquite tree sap mixed with another substance which is unknown to me to this day. Then he taped it up with a strong cloth tape and stuffed the shaft of the boot with rags. Next came the deep freezer for three days or so, and after thawing out, it fit better than ever. I still have the boots and they still fit.

Dad kept my gear when I went in the Navy. I guess he figured I would want it all when I got back home. He was right of course but things changed while I was gone and I came back home with a pregnant wife. Rodeo was not a thing I thought would provide a paycheck for two people to live on. I wanted to get an education and I needed a job.

That's a story I will tell at another time. I just let the dream of riding horses fade away and drift off into the past. I still wanted to remember those days and those times with Billy but my new little family and my drive to survive took over and I moved on from bronc riding. Those were indeed the days of high adventure for a skinny kid from Yuma.

Little Brother

She told me she liked me and wanted to get to know me better. We were friends at school and she actually talked to me in front of others, which I found to be an admirable quality for a young girl of my age. She was pretty and had a very nice figure for the age of 12. She lived near me and we would see each other at the stores around the area. Sometimes she would come to the A.J. Bayless Grocery Store where I worked after school and on some weekends. That is when I wasn't off with my brother doing our horse thing.

We talked about getting together and going to a movie or getting a burger together. We figured it would take some planning 'cause neither one of us had a car. What we did have were bicycles and that would get the job done if not too far away, not too expensive, and not too late at night. It worked out fine 'cause her mom would drop her off at the movie theater downtown and I would get a lift from my brother or Mom. Then we could sit together to eat popcorn, drink cherry cokes, and even hold hands with each other like people do on a real date.

Mom liked her and thought she was a nice girl with good manners, that dressed well and kept herself clean and pretty. Her mother liked me and thought I was a nice boy that came from good upbringing and was well-groomed. My mother cut my hair 'til I was well into my teenage years and she only had one style for me: butch.

Turned out the girl had a problem with me and horses. Said it wasn't her thing to go to rodeo events and watch people do the same thing over and over again. I tried to tell her how I was working on getting better at what I did and that I liked doing it. She didn't like it and so we came to the parting of the ways. Sure wish life companions, as they would turn out to be later on in life, could be dealt with in such a simple and clean fashion. No marriage and no divorce, just spend time together, eat popcorn, drink cokes, and then go our separate ways without fighting or arguing about it. Kind of like the horses I would meet at an event. Ride for a very short while and then move on to the next and then the next. No commitment to anything except having fun and then moving on.

At school, the girl would speak to me and ask if I wanted to go to a movie or something, but I always had other things to do and so we drifted apart even at school. She said I loved my rodeo more than I loved anything else and she was right. Besides sitting in a dark movie show wasn't my idea of fun. I needed to be out in the fresh air wearing boots and a hat, that's where my interest was at the age I had achieved.

She told me I didn't have any school spirit. I didn't get involved in sports activities, I didn't attend sports rallies, I didn't go to sporting events involving the school teams, and I was always gone doing my riding. I said she was right on every count and that I was not about to change for her or anyone. I had decided to live my life my way and told her she could live her life her way. For some reason, this seemed to draw her closer to me.

But then came the summer break from school and I didn't see her 'til the start of the following school year as freshmen in high school. She acted like she didn't know me at all and was busy with her friends in Glee Club and cheerleading. I kept busy with my job at the grocery store and doing my riding whenever I got the chance and the girl just faded out of sight. Wish I could remember her name but I can't. I can't even find her picture in the school yearbook. But if you know anything about school yearbooks, the freshmen' pictures are very small and not at all what people really look like.

Speaking of not looking like they really are. Billy and I got to ride in the Silver Spur Rodeo Parade in Yuma many times over the years. He rode Duke who was used to crowds of people and noises of all kinds and I rode Zona, who was laid back and calm in all the excitement of people. I always wore my hat pulled down snug on my head and sunglasses. No one every knew who I was. Just like being a nobody teenager in my own hometown. It was all part of the Yuma Junior Chamber of Commerce group where Billy was a member. They didn't seem to mind me tagging along. Just another rider and nobody really.

Then there was Sandy. She came from California during my Junior school year and she was beautiful. Sandy always wore a lot of makeup which I did not understand because she was a very pretty girl without all that goop on her face. For some reason, she took a liking to me and spoke to me all the time. We had classes together and she didn't mind being seen with me at breaks and at lunch. Sandy was very active in Cheerleading, Girls' Sports, and Drama Club. She was fast becoming a very popular girl in our school. We never did date or do anything outside of school but I always thought I was somewhat a normal boy because she seemed to care about me while others did not. Sandy came to my house once to see me when I had called in sick to school. Said she didn't see me for several days and wondered how I was doing. I actually had bruised my right hip so bad over the past weekend in an event that I couldn't walk. Sandy was a very nice and caring person.

I have often wondered about Sandy over the years after high school. I hope she turned out to be a well-rounded person in life and found her own fame and fortune. As far as I know Sandy never did attend a rodeo event. Never attended one with me as the main attraction that I know of that is.

Pam was a redheaded girl with freckles and cute as a bug's ear. She saw me at the rodeo over in Brawley and even spoke to me there. Said her name was Pam and that we had classes together at Kofa. She asked if this was something new for me or had I been doing this for a while. I told her I'd been rough stock riding for a few years and hoped to get better as I went. She said she loved rodeo and being around the stock more than anything.

In the time we had together, we talked about school and some of the other kids we knew. She said she would never have known I was doing this sport if she had not been there to see it. I asked her to not make a big deal of it and if she could please don't talk about me at school. I just wanted to stay out of anyone's headlights if I could. I sure would appreciate it if she could do that. She said she would and decided it would be our secret.

Pam and I got along fine at school and I always informed her about events in and around the state and in California. Sometimes she would show up at the place other times not. I often thought if I took the time Pam and I could have been closer than we were. It never happened. I found out some years later that Pam was killed in a car wreck on the road to San Diego. If we had hooked up would she not have been in that car? Would I have been in that car with her? Life has a way of defining who we are and how we live even without our knowing it.

At the annual Silver Spur Rodeo in Yuma, the Rodeo Announcer knew me and Billy very well, and over the loud speaker would say every contestant's name as they were about to enter an event. When it came my turn to ride, he would invariably announce me as "Little Brother" to let people know I was Billy's little brother. I didn't mind and it seemed to be all right with everyone else as well. Little Brother, as I was known to all, seemed to fit me. Turns out the announcer was the same guy in Wellton, Somerton, Brawley, Nogales, and Prescott.

Even after 50 years had passed Billy still called me Little Brother. It was a name I earned and was proud to wear even if only to my big brother Billy and that rodeo announcer. We would joke with each other back in those rodeo days and I would call Billy "Big" and he would call me "Little". It was our way of acknowledging each other and the status and affection we held for one another. I always wanted to be like Billy, until he had his stroke, and even then he was always Big Brother. Billy passed away in 2011 and with him went the close tie we both shared in those rowdy days back in Yuma.

Seems that chasing that dream of the perfect ride was just in fact a dream and never really became real. Dreams live on while fame and fortune fade over time or so they say. I wouldn't know about the fame and fortune part. Dreams last a lifetime and more.

Liniment

It seems here of late, that life is a series of bad backs. I seem to go from one to another and back again. I would like to strengthen my back a bit to avoid the back attacks, but it seems that my attempts are thwarted by another bout of bad back. If I do nothing in a few days I'm fine, If I try to do something I only make it worse. I do not see a winning combination of doing nothin and doing something. It all stems from a back injury I suffered as a boy upon hitting the earth from a height of about 10 feet as I was coming off the back of a particularly rank horse in a timed event. As I recall I couldn't walk after that incident for about a week or so. It was my first of many bad back attacks along with the broken ribs that so often seem to accompany the back pain. At the time getting bent and bruised was all part of the sport we were playing with horses in the hunt for a shiny piece of metal used to hold our britches up. For me, that would be Little Britches Rodeo events and as it went, there was no money in it, just pain and an occasional pat on the back for a job well done.

For some reason going to the events even hurt and being unable to ride was always the first thing on my mind. The other boys were always glad to see ya even if you couldn't compete, or maybe because of it. I didn't miss too many go-arounds at the rodeo's that I went to. Even hurt there was always the drive to get up and do the deed, sometimes even without the use of a good hand. Trying to be a Top Hand was first and foremost at what I did for a hobby.

It seemed the girls that had any interest in me at these gatherings were older than I and I didn't like it at all. For some reason, they must have thought I was interested in them cause my mother always taught me to be nice and polite to them. But the truth of the matter was that I didn't want any attention from them and really wanted them to leave me alone. It was the same at age 12 on up to 16 years old for me. Then one day I did notice a girl and she seemed to show some interest in me as well. She did not know I was in

65

school with her and had been for several years but that's the way it was for me. Always a nobody and virtually invisible to everyone.

I actually talked to her and she talked to me. She asked me about the smell I seemed to have and I told her it was some medicine for my sore back and she said it was not a pleasant smell. Then I had to do my thing at the rodeo and that was that for that girl. In school, she did not know who I was or that we had talked. I sure did not know how to impress the girls. At the start of this piece, I was talking about my bad back and how it always seemed to come to me when I least expected it and really for doing nothing to get it. Anyone who has had a bad back knows how disabling a thing it can be. You can do some things but it hurts, you can't do somethings and it still hurts, and no position is ever comfortable. I have tried cold compresses and heating pads and salves of every kind. Once my brother Billy put some horse liniment on me and all it did was set my world on fire. He was very specific that I should not allow the stuff to run down the crack of my butt cheeks and get to my water-tight door. He said that would be a disaster in the first degree. When I asked him he said the stuff was good for Duke (his horse) so it had to be good for me. I knew he was right. The smell of the liniment on your person was not something that went away quickly and people at school did not appreciate me coming around smelling up the place. So no matter how good a job it would do to elevate pain I did not use the stuff if I was going to school. Sometimes old injuries compounded by new injuries would just get a good boy down. No school and nothing else, just a lot of laying around to get healed up and able to walk upright again.

Here we are some 55 years later and it still hurts when it comes back to haunt me.

Nothing I can do to keep it away, it just comes. Brother Billy said I would have to pay the piper and that piper bastard has held a heavy debt over my head for a lot of years. They say if you wake up pain-free you're dead. I have gone through growing pains, heart ache pains, and pains of loss with family and friends, and the pains all get better with time. In this world I have decided that time stays the same, it is people that change. They come and they go but time is constant. So too is my aching back.

Billy told me if I got good at rodeo, I could make a name for myself. I said I already have a name and don't need another. As it turns out I did make a name for myself in my little world but no one knew it but me. In my mind, I was a world-champion bronc rider. In my mind, I was a lot of things. But then my normal isn't your normal. Hell, my normal isn't anybody's normal. Normal doesn't really have a firm definition that can be used for everyone.

When mom was living in her assisted living home Billy and I would spend time with her. We loved being able to care for her in her declining years. Billy had a stroke in 2003 and was single at the time. Living then in Lake Havasu City he would drive his car to Chandler to see mom at least once if not twice a month. The trip was three hours one way and he did it with the use of only his left arm and left leg. During those visits Billy and I would talk about our time together and how we did back then with horses. It seemed to help him as if it were some kind of Liniment being put on a painful part of the soul. He always missed his horse Duke and the times they had together. They really were a fantastic duo in the roping arena. Sometimes Billy would get all teary-eyed and sad about those by gone days. I remember asking him if there was one thing he would like to do over again and had that ability, what would it be? Billy told me he would just love to sit on Duke again for one more time and ride off into the great unknown. In 2011 Billy did just that and I was there to hold his hand as he made his escape from this life. I miss him with all my heart but I also know that his memories are the Liniment I need for living.

Just a Boy in Yuma

5 or 6 Years Old

When I was a boy in Yuma, I used to say "I can ride that" which meant it was good, or "I can't ride that" which meant that it was bad. It always seemed to me being alone was easy, cause there was no one there to butt in on your activity. I always had something to do as a kid, I never had a dull moment in my backyard, and always had a plan for the day. Moving dirt was a major force for me and I had plenty of it to move from one place to another with my Tonka Dump Truck. Spud, my dog was always there to help and to watch as I worked at my job, keeping constant vigil over my work site.

As the years rolled on I got into caring for horses with my brother Billy. Spud didn't see me then every day all day long and he missed me. Seemed like the care of these larger animals took more time than I ever imagined, and then of course I started going to Roping Events with Billy. That was often but not all the time, and I still had my chores to do with the horses down at Don's place, which I got paid for.

16 Years Old

At sixteen years I had my own car, a 1940 Chevrolet Coupe. Very nice car for me, brand new motor and transmission. With the car, I could take Spud with me down to see the animals at Don's place. The Rodeo events that I attended in those early years did not lend themselves to my driving my own car. Getting busted up was not good for driving a car. Billy too, got banged up once in a while but not so often, so he did the driving for the most part.

After a while, I began to realize that what I was doing was not appreciated by anyone as much as me. My skill level was rising and I was getting more confident as the events came and went.

I kept my eye on the goal by trying harder to get better and it was paying off. Billy of course was there to tell me not to get cocky and careless, or I'd end up getting hurt bad. I told him from what I could see this sport is all about getting hurt real bad every time I climb aboard one of these rank broncs. And of course, Billy was always there to tell me to "put dirt on it and don't tell Mom". With regards to those words which I have carried all my life, I have found them best used in dealing with women. Riding broncs was a physical hurt along with the hurt in pride, but with women, the pain lasted longer and cost more by a long shot. What women say they are going to do, and what they actually do, are not even in the same arena. Not the women I have so carelessly joined up with.

Billy told me the memories I am making are mine alone and that I should work at never losing them. I have worked at keeping them intact all of my life. I have shared some with others and some I have never shared and never will. I find peace in this life by going back in time to those special days and nights of my youth. They are the purest times of life for me. You can bet Billy, Duke, and Spud are there with me in those times. A young skinny kid with eagerness shining through blue eyes for the next wild adventure.

Had an old barbell set on the back porch at that house in Yuma, and I worked lifting it every way I could to build muscle so I could compete better. I tried as best I could to get stronger, and Spud was my cheerleader. Billy said running would do me a lot of good in my training routine, so I did that a lot. In my world of running, I got the idea to wear my boots and wranglers to go up and down the sand hills near my home, and it was very difficult to do. The hills were steep, and the sand was deep, but I wanted to keep doing it to get stranger. Turns out it was the most difficult thing I have ever tried to do. Many a time I just couldn't make myself do it, other times I could do it with ease. Because of this plan to get stronger, I found that I did indeed get stronger, and my bronc riding improved greatly. Riding rank horses was a mind game but having stronger legs and back made it a lot more manageable.

Billy told me about horses from what he had already learned. Horses you see are right or left-handed. Most males are left-handed while most females are right-handed. Not always the case but pretty much that way. So they have a strong side and a weak side, just like we do. A lead side as it turns out, and a way to move in that direction side. He told me about the whorls on the horses, which can be found on the face, stifle, belly, neckline, and chest. The use of these cowlicks can indicate the temperament of the animal. It can also lead itself to telling right or left handiness in the animal. Clockwise being mostly right-handed and counterclockwise being mostly left-handed. But he said it's all a guess but narrows the field a good deal to know about it. Duke as it turned out was ambidextrous which in a roping horse was most outstanding.

I remember being over at the Brawley, California Cattle Call Rodeo must a been 1963 or so November of that year. Won a buckle but paid dearly for it. Momma was out of her mind with hurt and anger over the deal. Wasn't much I could hide, my shirt was tattered, and my wranglers were torn, couldn't walk straight, it hurt to breathe, those old boys at the Rodeo taped me up like a G.D. mummy and told me to go to the Yuma Hospital when we got back to town if I was still among the living. I did live, and I did go to the Hospital, they said take it easy - Wow Solid Medical Advice for sure. No school for me had to lay around home for a couple weeks. That Buckle didn't seem worth all the misery it brought. I kept thinking I could do better next time, and for sure there would be a next time.

That Which is Allowed

The Sun was always up before I was in my growing-up years. Warm would be the operative word for the Sun in the morning in Yuma. By nine o'clock it would burn you to stand in it without moving and by noon it would fry you to a cinder if you allowed. A place in the Sun was never the place I wanted to be. Sunbathing in Yuma is directly proportional to one's inability to understand man's place in the Sun. Being barefoot in Yuma is a thing done one time and even then is short-lived. Grass, if it can be found in Yuma, will burn your feet if you walk on it without foot protection.

Sandstorms in Yuma are a very real occurrence and happen often. The sand being blown by the wind can and does etch glass, damage chrome, cut into brick and stone, and remove paint completely. Our house in Yuma was built of brick and often needed to be repainted in certain areas due to the sandstorms. I always wanted to help my father do the painting that he felt was needed. He always wanted the house to be white in color. So, we painted the house using white paint. I once asked him if we could paint the house gray to match the color of the bricks and then as the sand removed the paint, we couldn't see that the paint was missing cause it would be the same color as the paint. His answer as always was simple and easy to hear. No, and that was it, end of conversation.

Growing up in that house in Yuma came with summers in the range of 110 to 120 degrees in the shade. My father believed in Evaporative Coolers to keep the house cool inside at minimal use of electricity. I remember him installing the first of many units on our roof over the years as they would rot out or fall apart. The last unit was a fiberglass housing with the same type of internal watering parts and a motor with a belt and large drum turned to send cool air inside the house. Evaporation cooling works just fine until the humidity gets high enough to stop the effects of evaporation. That came in August almost every year and we lived through it as best we could. Years later Dad had an Air Conditioner installed and he and Mom enjoyed that for many years. I was gone from home by that time and upon returning for a visit here and there it was a real treat to know that Mom and Dad had moved into the modern age.

In all the years living there in that town, I never saw a person actually trying to get a suntan by laying in the sun. Everyone who wore shorts had tanned legs. Short sleeved shirt meant tanned arms. Not wearing a hat meant a burned head and skin cancer on your ears for sure. It made perfect sense to stay out of the sun whenever possible, and not doing so meant burning. Such was the life we lived in that environment.

The water in Yuma was so hard and brackish that you could almost chew it right from the tap. Life in that desert town was like the tap water, harsh but livable. Never had allergies as a kid growing up there. The wind would blow any and all pollen away every day. The wind would blow away everything in time. Even memories if you didn't hold onto them tightly.

I remember a car dealership in Yuma, Donkersley Studebaker. They sold Studebaker Cars and International Harvester Trucks. In 1962 they advertised all over that little town about their newest model car The Avanti. They had a big party at their dealership. They had pony rides for the kids, face painting, balloons, Hot Dogs, and Hamburgers. They spent a lot of money promoting the new car. It really was a beauty of a sleek four-passenger sports car. Fiberglass body and 260 Cubic Inch Engine, it was the hot new car to see for sure. Over the course of a three-day weekend offering, they spent a lot of money to get people to come down to see the new car, which they did. After all was said and done not one of the new cars of which they only had one, was sold. The following year did not do any better, and the only time the Avanti was seen on the streets of Yuma it was being driven by one of the salesmen from the dealership. One good thing did come of all the hype about the new car. The dealership sold more International Trucks than ever before. Yuma was a truck town for sure.

1961 I was in the market for my first car. I found a 1958 Studebaker Silver Hawk for sale and drove it down to show my father at the fire station where he was on duty. I remember the car was Black and Gold in color and sat very low to the ground. The engine was large being a 260 Cubic Inch with a four-speed transmission. My father said that car would be my demise as it was fast and I would drive it fast without even knowing it.

The car had a lot of miles on it, had leaks in the engine, and the exhaust was very loud. Without Dad's approval, I took the car back to the owner and said no deal. I don't remember how much was being asked for the car but it was not a consideration and I moved on in my search.

1940 Chevrolet

In the little town where I grew up, there were few cars to choose from as a boy of 15 rapidly approaching that magical age of 16. At 16 boys started moving into that realm held sacred by all adult males, that being the realm of the driving person. Obtaining a Driver's License was, without a doubt, the second step towards manhood you know. I already had taken the first step to manhood, I knew how to smoke cigarettes, so I would really be on my way when I got my driver's License. I was intent on one thing for sure, to find a car that I could afford. As luck would have it I stumbled onto a 1940 Chevrolet Coupe in very good shape but with a motor that was just worn out. I purchased the car in running order for $85.00 and drove it home. Mind you I didn't have a driver's license yet. That's when that old adage, putting the horse before the cart, came into play. I told my dad that I needed this car to take the test to get my license. After looking it over he said I would be lucky to go around the block with this thing. Then there was the matter of the title to the car and me being 15 years old, getting insurance on the car and me being 15 years old, but first I needed to pass the test for the driver's license. Title, insurance and all that was just secondary to the real prize of getting that driver's License. Hey, I know what you're thinking but I had a job that paid something, and it was after school and weekends at the A J Bayless grocery store as a stock clerk. I didn't get any free handouts from my folks to keep my car running. Discount on insurance thanks to the Driver Education course at school, discount on cigarettes at the grocery store, and gas money coming in what more could a guy want?

I was in Auto Shop in school you know so I decided I needed to make this car a dream come true. The first thing I did was yank that old 216 Cast Iron six-cylinder motor out of the old girl, along with the vacuum shift 3-speed transmission. Next came the selection process of finding a replacement motor for my soon-to-be car of a real man. A complete and thorough search of the junk yards around town came down to the perfect, even if the only, selection. A 1958 Oldsmobile had been totaled in a rollover wreck in which three people had died. If I could take the engine out of the wreck, I could have it for $50.00. One Saturday with three buddies working on it, we had a motor for the old girl. A 1958 Oldsmobile 354 V-8 and brother, I was cooking. The next major obstacle was how to put this motor into that car. The second major obstacle was to find a transmission that would adapt to this motor. Hey, remember I'm 15 going on manhood, no problem with these small things. First of all, I had to rebuild the Olds Motor for my class project. Main Bearings on up through the Heads, porting and polishing as we went. That's when I realized how much the parts cost and how expensive they would be if I broke them by misuse. Reinforcing the frame to hold the engine wasn't easy. Moving fenders to make room was a real challenge and keep the same outside look. We had to redo the front end completely with new steering and struts. A friend gave me what he thought was a Buick Road Master Transmission with broken gears. Turned out to be a 1937 LaSalle and after many hours I found through mail order some Lincoln Zephyr Gears for it. And they cost a lot too. Next, we went back to the junkyard and found a Thunderbird rear end which we could adapt to this frame. After all, was said and done I had a 1940 Chevrolet Coupe Deluxe with a 1958 Oldsmobile 354 Motor which I had punched up a bit, a 1937 LaSalle Transmission with Lincoln gears, a 1939 Ford Truck Clutch Pack, and a 1959 Ford Thunderbird Rear End. I had a set of used 10 hundred 16 slicks on the rear, Glass Pack Mufflers, an Electric Fuel Pump, and a custom-made large core radiator to keep her cool. The tan and white Diamond Tuck and Roll did the interior up real good and I even got the old radio in the dash working with speakers in the door panels. This was a Rocket waiting for the launch date. Some bodywork here and there and a slick paint job of 1954 Oldsmobile Sierra Gold over a White undercoat and man I was the talk of the town. On my initial voyage with the rocket, I punched the drive line right through the gas tank and floorboard. How I didn't destroy the whole car is amazing to me. Had the drive line re-measured and lathed, moved the gas tank, and worked on using the 1200-pound clutch with no hydraulic slave unit. Man, this thing could literally fly.

The year was 1962 and the fastest car in town was a Red 1962 Pontiac Bonneville. The second fastest was a 1939 Mercury with a beefed-up motor.

I decided I would take on the Mercury, cause I knew him and he wasn't out to dominate the world. First race I missed second gear and still beat him.

Second run at him I really beat him bad. Now the word got out to the guy with the Red Pontiac and we were destined to clash. I had figured out that destroying my dream car was the last thing I wanted to do and that racing it was the fastest way to do just that. Now in those days being labeled a chicken was no way to be. Besides people felt that by building something like this you were into racing and putting your life on the line for the glory of the sport. Hey, remember when I started this piece I was 15 years old looking forward to the day I would turn 16 years old and get a driver's license. So along came my 16th Birthday and I got my license to drive. Figured out how to save money on insurance by taking the Driving Class in school which took forever. Got through that and obtained the basic coverage so if I killed someone my coverage would send them flowers.

For a year I avoided contact with the infamous Red Pontiac, and that was no small feat considering who we were and where we lived. But at the age of almost 17 years I was not looking for fame as a racer I was looking for the next step toward manhood. That next step was finding out why I needed to be with a naked girl.

As luck would have it I was sent to detention one fine day for acting up in some manner deemed inappropriate, and while at the office chanced to meet a new girl just checking into school. She was very lovely although a bit heavy on the makeup and her name was Sandy. Sandy had what appeared to be a large and firm set of breasts for a girl of 17, and I was determined to get a closer look at them.

Sandy was from California and wanted to know if I had a car. I said yes. She wanted to know if I was going with anyone and if not would I take her to the drive-in on Friday night? I said yes. She told me where she lived and said to pick her up at 7. I said yes. Boy oh boy, here I was about to get the chance of a lifetime to move to that third and final step toward manhood.

Sex was knocking at my door and I figured if I played my cards right the front seat of my 40 Chevy would be the springboard to heaven on Friday night at the drive-in movie. Good looking guy, cherry car, drive-in movie, plus a willing girl, a winning combination in any game of chance.

Then life, as we know it, will steps in and throw us a curve ball. I mentioned earlier about being sent to detention for inappropriate behavior. Well, it seems my mother got wind of this and I was grounded for two weeks. Had to walk to school and back, but worst of all Friday night and the chance to see Sandy naked was gone. Later in life, I found out that the Aborigines don't have a concept of tomorrow or future. If you lock them up they will die. I knew then how they feel but just how bad it was didn't hit me until later. It turns out that Sandy was a girl on the move and she found several other interested guys to take her out not only on that fateful Friday night but every other Friday night for some time. My first lesson in the ways of romance was to hear how she was a slut and would do anybody and was intent on proving it. The problem for me was that the guy she decided to hook up with finally was the guy that drove that Red 1962 Pontiac.

Call it immaturity, call it stupid, no matter what you may say, I figured that if I wanted my shot with Sandy if I really wanted to see her naked on the front seat of my car, I would have to do battle with the guy with the Red Pontiac. It never occurred to me that I would lose a race against him. It never occurred to me that even if I did beat him, Sandy would stay with him. None of this logic was even a factor in my thinking. What was a factor was the thought of moving onward in my quest for ultimate manhood and reaching that plateau as soon as possible. Then in steps fate again and everything takes a turn in another direction.

My mother introduced me to a girl named Susan. Susan went to the other high school in town and was the daughter of one of Mom's church friends.

I was taken by her charm, and she was all smiles with me. Susan was well endowed and cute in a small girl kind of way. We went on a date, and I found out what was missing in my young life. Susan liked me for a while, but she was moving onward and upward also and soon lost interest in me. Thanks to Susan, I had reached that third step toward manhood, but it just didn't mean what I thought it would mean. I had lost interest in Sandy, and what I thought she had the exclusive market on. I started looking at the opposite sex differently and started seeing the women mixed in with the girls. They hadn't changed but I had. Sports was a great outlet for all the frustration that I was feeling in those pivotal years before manhood, but a girlfriend that was popular and good-looking too, that would be a dream come true. Then came Sandra. I even noticed then that the girls in my life so far had names that started with S. Sandra was beautiful, talented, smart, and very popular. What she saw in me was anybody's guess. She wasn't interested in helping me get better at the art of sex, as a matter of fact, she wasn't interested in me at all. I had a car and that was enough for her but not for me. I needed to get on with the search for the perfect girlfriend and I had a couple of prospects in line.

Ω

Riding My Dreams

Last Exit to Yuma

From my earliest days in Yuma, I was aware of the gift of space and time. Growing up in that small town I was a loner and did things that only loners do. School was not of interest to me as a boy in that town. I walked to school and sat in the classroom, and then walked home. Nothing of importance ever happened in those years. I don't remember teachers, or classrooms, or other kids. It's as if I just grew up alone.

I had a dog, and I had a rifle, that's all there was of interest to me as a boy at that time. I grew up without Television or Radio. If I wasn't outside in the Sun, then I wasn't doing anything. I didn't care about books or schoolwork, they meant nothing to me. At recess, I would walk around the perimeter of the schoolyard and look off into the neighborhoods that surrounded the school to see what was out there. I wanted to be out there and not in the schoolyard. I had homework and I did it at the kitchen table, but I don't remember it being of any interest to me. I never once looked forward to going to school, and I never once spoke out or joined in the school classroom events. My report card always said that I don't speak to and don't socialize with the other students. I maintained my own space and kept it to myself.

My teachers always thought I was a slow learner and perhaps a bit retarded. I didn't care what they thought. I didn't want what they had to offer and getting smarter was not a goal of mine. When they would have a parent conference with my mother, they would say that I was lagging in the classroom and not participating with the other kids. I didn't have any friends in school and seemed withdrawn from joining in with anything. When they asked me about it I would say I wasn't interested in school or in participating. I told them I would rather not go to school and just stay home with my dog.

My brother Billy got me into Rodeo, and I found that I could do that and get good at it, so I did. Rodeo never involved the kids at school, and it was something I could do on my own with only one teacher and that was Billy my older brother.

To this day I remember walking those sand-covered streets of Yuma as a kid. I saw all of the emotions of man from Love to Rage. I saw people at their lowest and their highest bordering on hope, fulfillment, fear, defeat, and destruction. I finally made it out of Yuma after 18 years before falling into the complacency of life in that community. I know that to truly live you have to experience death up close and personal. There and in other places that I lived and worked in years to come, I did just that. I could see the road that lay ahead of me and I was eager to get on it and move into the future. Moving away from Yuma, was also on the agenda I had set before me. I made that happen as soon as I could.

Phase Two of my life was the United States Navy and at 18 years old I made that event happen, the year was 1965. New places, new people, new adventures, all new things to do. None of it was of much interest to me when it was happening. Patrol Squadron, Aircrew Man, Hawaii, Alaska, all points East, and it was just beginning to get interesting when it all ended. Made it to E 5 Petty Officer Second Class, and my rate was Anti Submarine Warfare Technician had earned my Aircrew Wings and a hand full of medals and decided to end my adventure in the Navy. So I mustered out of the Navy in January 1969 with my belongings and a life partner, Gwendolyn.

Phase Three of my life was the Tempe Police Department and at age 22 years old I began my transition to Police Officer. Had a wife as of January 1969, and started learning to care for someone else as well as myself. She was pregnant and due in August. I had never made anything of importance in my life and was excited to see the child she was carrying. It was a girl and we named her Kelly. It was a rough infancy for Kelly. She had seizures often and we had to be aware of her not breathing and convulsing most every day. This went on for a year and then stopped. She was a delightful little partner for me and as I became the cold callous Policeman that I needed to be she kept me grounded with family and love.

From 1969 to 1976 it was me and Kelly and Gwen. We did all the things a family could do together and loved each other without limits. Then in 1976 along came Autumn, a sister to Kelly and another little girl for me. Kelly absolutely took over caring for Autumn, and it seemed Autumn was Kelly's little girl, not Gwen's. Our family was indeed growing.

Phase Four of my life was to begin in 1977 when I stopped being a Police Officer and was hired on at United Parcel Service as a Delivery Driver. Kelly was 8 years old, Autumn was 1 year old, and Gwen and I were just getting to know each other well. The next 8 years were a blur of marriage, growing little girls, and Gwen growing in interest away from family. I was busy as a UPS Driver and didn't see it coming. I just didn't see it coming at all.

Phase Five of my life began on January 1, 1985. Gwen walked out of my life and drove away, never to return. I don't love you anymore, I don't want to live with you anymore, and I want a divorce, were the words she used to me. I was devastated and hurt but kept going as if it was really not happening and of course, I was in denial.

Denial very quickly grew into Anger. I was hurt but I was fighting mad also. That woman could just leave me and the girls alone, go off with her new lover, and set up house with him and not us. Turns out she had already done those things about setting up house with him and that leaving me was the last thing she had to do. A clean break was her plan and it worked very well for her. Being the last one to know, I was of course hopeful that this was just a phase and things would get back to normal in no time. This, as it turned out, was to be the new normal and nothing would ever be the old normal again. 16 years of marriage ended in one moment in time. One month into the separation I filed for divorce, and the bargaining ran its course in the courts to end in August. I was depressed to a certain degree, but that quickly moved into acceptance and the realization that my girls were still my girls and that my wife was no longer my wife, just a woman I spent time with for a number of years. I took a girlfriend for 2 1/2 years and when that ended I was on my own to find out who I was. That relationship was so unimportant to me that I am not even going to mention her name.

During the years between 1985 and 2006, I made a great many mistakes with women and my life. Suffice it to say they do not deserve any further comment in this narrative. Never have and never will. I had made bad choices and like falling off a horse I had to get back up and get back on.

Phase Six of my life began in 2007 when I retired from United Parcel Service and began to live life alone. 30 years with UPS was enough and I wanted out and away. That summer at the coaxing of a friend I returned to College to get my degree. Left ASU in 1977 when I stopped being a Police Officer and began my career as a UPS Driver.

Needed 4 hours to graduate and acquire my degree in Criminal Justice. Didn't see the point in pursuing that degree in 1977 as I was no longer a Police Officer and United Parcel Service didn't care if I had a degree or not. I didn't care as well. For 30 years they didn't care and I didn't care. But back to school I went, cause I didn't have anything to do with myself, and going back to college seemed like the right thing to do. Got the degree and have it proudly hung on a wall in my home. Made my Momma happy to know I did that. Got to check that item off my bucket list and didn't even know it was on my bucket list.

Phase Seven - Georgia - Lucky Number for me. Georgia began work at United Parcel Service in 1999 and over the years till 2007, we worked together and apart. Our relationship had its ups and down's but through it all, we stayed sociable and seemed to enjoy each other's input in our daily work and our separate and uniquely different lives. Georgia was and had been married for 27 years with four kids and according to her she was happily married and planned to stay that way. I grew to love her and cherished the time I was allowed to spend with her always at work and never away from that environment. I was divorced and living alone in 2006 and saw that as the way I was going to stay for many years to come. Georgia was what I wanted but felt it would never be.

Phase Eight - Retirement - After I left UPS in 2007 I spent my time out in the desert hunting and fishing with my dog at the time Bugs. Bugs was my pal and had been in my house since about 2002 or so, and we went everywhere together. 2007 was also the year I learned that Georgia was not happily married as she had said and in fact was getting out of her abusive relationship with a man who had proven over and over to be a drunk, a dope smoker, and addicted to porn. I was told about this through a letter she sent me. I could see the door of our relationship slowly opening and I was ready for it to happen.

Serious relationships for me over the years have never been good and ended up badly. I wanted my desires to be justified and more than just the acts of a lonely man in search of a mate for a short time. I needed to ease into this relationship, if indeed Georgia was going to allow such a thing to happen, and be certain of who she was and what she meant to me. For several months we socialized and went to events and places together. She got to meet my kids and I sort of met some of her kids, although that was going to prove to be a difficult hurdle to overcome. Her kids thought she divorced them, not their father. They also thought I was the other man who took her affection away from their father. Not really on point with their surmise of the situation, but I didn't give a rip about what they thought. My kids accepted Georgia for the person they knew she was and that has never changed. I grew to know her better over time and realized this was the person I wanted to spend the rest of my life with. Georgia also decided the same with me so in 2008 we tied the knot and moved our two lives into one house. We began our marriage committed to each other and also decided to respect each other and treat each other better than we had ever treated anyone in our lives. We are kind and loving to each other without pretense every moment we are together, which is almost 24 hours a day every day. Together we have dealt with Billy my brother and his needs till his passing. My mother and her living arraignments till her passing. Together we weathered the loss of our little buddy Bugs and have learned to deal with the emptiness without them in our lives. Georgia's children have not fully accepted me yet, but they are more tolerant of my presence in their mother's life. It's slow going.

Georgia has taken on new and varied responsibilities in her personal life. New business ventures, new friends, and even new spiritual growth with me. I moved her to Prescott from Chandler in 2014 to get out of Phoenix, the heat of summer, the traffic, and the crime. We have now adapted to the climate and the weather changes. The smaller town of Prescott is perfect for us and we love it. My health issues have been a rocky road at times but together we have made it through to where we are now in 2019.

I don't know what the future holds for us, no one does. What we do know with every bit of certainty is that we have a rare gift from God with each other. It is the affection and love we share for one another that will get us down the road we are on together. So far so good and it will only get better. In God we trust.

Since leaving Yuma so many years ago I have never wanted to go back there for anything. My work took me there often for short periods of time and I found that to be acceptable. When I moved Mom to Chandler, Arizona to live in 2007 and sold the family house I never wanted to go back.

I've been told that our view of God has a great deal to do with our growing-up years and the view we hold of our earthly father. The view I hold of my earthly father is personal and deep inside me. I miss my father and I miss my mother, but most of all I miss my Brother Billy. My feelings for Billy are the strongest feelings of all my family members, and if what I have been told is true, then my view of God is influenced by my view of my brother Billy and what we accomplished together with horses.

I always believed that Yuma was something that was endured, hard-fought, painful, and buried deep inside me and covered by the sands of time. It has taken me almost a full lifetime to realize that when I got hurt and my brother Billy said "Put dirt on it and don't tell mom." He said the dirt I put on my hurts was the magical dirt of Yuma. I have always had that magical dirt with me to soothe me after a fall.

It is the last exit to Yuma, that I watch for on this highway of life that I am on. I know where it is and I have a ticket to ride that train down at the Yuma Train Depot if I so desire but I don't want to go there. At least not just yet.

Nothing in Yuma is any part of my life today, nothing that is alive anyway. I closed that door years ago and it will remain locked for me as I have intentionally misplaced the Key. Regarding that Train Depot in Yuma, I am reminded of a Poem I wrote at the time of my father's passing. In it, I refer to that Glory Bound Train we will all take someday when our time on this earth is over. I include it here and hope it helps the reader understand me a bit more.

Glory Bound Train

before dad left this world he said he knew Jesus
and could hear his Lord calling him home
he knew in his heart that once he'd depart
that he would never again be alone
said he had his ticket all paid up in full
to board that glory-bound train
it was leaving at dawn and he said he'd be on
next stop to see momma again
he looked up from bed and smiled as he said
son, do you have your ticket in hand
will it get you aboard that glory-bound train
and allow me to see you again
I told him yes sir I'm going there too
but it'll take a little bit longer
I'll be there to board that glory-bound train
my faith couldn't be any stronger
alright then I'll go but I'll be at the door
on the platform down at the station
where the glory bound train drops us all off

Riding My Dreams

to meet and greet our relations
in this world, we're alone without train fare home
no ticket, no money, no pass
to get where we're going we need to believe
with faith in our Lord that will last
I'll be going aboard that glory-bound train
dad, as soon as our master calls me
I've got my ticket right here in my hand
my faith in my God assures me
Ω

Summer in Yuma

Sitting on the front porch of that old place on Orange Avenue. 5 years old at that time in my life and can see it as plain today as if I was there right now. The street light is on right in from of our house and the bugs are flying. Billy and Jimmy are both using ball bats to tee off on those flying critters and doing a real good job of hitting home runs. Dad with his pipe lit would sit and watch us boys as the radio played a baseball game from just inside the front window screen. Mom would be in the kitchen cleaning up after supper. As for me, I would be taking the whole thing in as I often did from my place on that porch. Watching the cars drive by and listening to the game with Dad, was life at its best. Sometimes we had a breeze, but most likely not and they were the kinds of hot summer nights that seem to burn into my memories for life.

Then Mom would come out to the porch with a hot cup of coffee for Dad, and sit in his lap as they talked so low to each other that I could not hear them. Just to see them together and see how they touched and talked, you knew they were in love and I mean in love with life. Usually, the game would end by 9:00 pm unless it went into extra innings, and it was time for us to go inside and get to the business of calling it a day. It might have been summer and no school days but rules were rules and we all followed them. Most nights were spent with us out back on wooden beds made by Dad for sleeping under the stars. Mom would hang wet sheets on lines around us to cool the evening breeze. There was always the smell of Turpentine in the cans the bedposts were in to keep crawling critters away from us. Nothing compares to sleeping outside with nothing but a sheet to cover up with. Mornings Dad was always up first to check the area around our beds for unwanted guests that would sometimes join us during the night. Then came the smell of Mom's cooking and fresh coffee brewing on the stove of that little house on Orange Avenue.

Knew a girl there in Yuma, her name was Betsy Middleton and she lived with her family down in the valley just past Ruby's Furniture on County E Street. We had known each other since we were old enough to know it and were best of friends at church and other events around town. Once in a while, she would spend the night with us in the summer and sleep out with us on our beds in the backyard. That meant Billy or Jimmy would sleep inside for that night to allow for that to happen. She always loved doing that with us

cause we lived up on the little mesa from the valley and did not have hardly any mosquitoes to speak of. Betsy was always a smart girl and planned to go far with her education and be someone of importance. We went to different schools all of our years in Yuma and only saw each other at church. I always considered her to be the sister that I never had, and in due time we drifted apart and I think the last time I saw her was about 1958. I have often wondered how my sister from another family turned out in life.

Market Place

I remember the open-air market down the street from where we lived on Orange Avenue. They had a canvas tarp stretched over the marketplace and a larger-than-life eval cooler blowing somewhat cool air throughout.

They had fresh produce and cold beer for everyone. Produce was cheap and fresh I don't think my mother ever paid more than two dollars for what she wanted. Cold Beer was $.25 and always in a bottle. Brands ranged from A-1 to Regal Pale to Falstaff to Pearl. My father always had a cold beer at the marketplace while looking at the produce and fruit. Melons were plentiful and right out of the fields that very day. There was a section that always took my attention and it had candy, nuts, and soda pop. Of course, there were women selling Tamales and Street Tacos, and they were the best ever.

We went there every week and usually walked from our house in the 700 block of Orange Avenue down to Third Street and Orange. Mom would take my Radio Flyer Wagon with us to haul back the groceries. We had an Ice Box in our house and Dad would get big blocks of ice from the Ice Plant down at 3rd Street and 9th Avenue for it. Paying attention to opening and closing the ice box kept the ice on hand for about a week. Every now and then we boys would get a piece of ice and man what a treat that was. On those occasions when Dad would make Ice Cream with the hand crank maker he would go get crushed ice down at the plant and he would of course use rock salt. I have never in my life after living 70+ years, ever tasted better Ice Cream than that which dad made at home with that hand crank Ice Cream maker. So good and so cold it was absolutely the best food man ever invented and I would take my oath on that.

Buddy

He always had a bag of Beechnut Chewing Tobacco hanging out of a pocket. One pant leg inside a boot, one pant leg outside. Boots were old, faded, and cracked Alligator Lizard skin leather. He wore a weathered and old light tan Stetson hat with a cattleman fold and a snake skin hatband. The hat was mostly the color of sweat and dirt. He wore a tarnished silver chain around his neck with a small silver locket. He wore western shirts, sleeves rolled up, and he always had creases in his faded Wranglers. He wore an old Rodeo Champion belt buckle made of silver and gold, rubies set in the corners. The buckle had to be 30 or 40 years old and well-worn. He was slight of build and stood about 5 foot 8 inches in his roper-style boots. Two fingers were missing off his right hand, little and ring fingers, but he still had a strong grip. Fingers were lost in WWII in the Pacific Theater of War. Bent and busted but getting around, he was a constant volunteer at the rodeos in and around the Yuma area. Age-wise he was in his 70s would have been my guess.

Buddy, was all I ever knew of his name, and for sure he was right friendly of character. Was said by folks that knew him he lived in a house down in the Yuma Valley. He drove a brand new Ford Pickup Truck with a lariat hanging in the back window and a bale or two of hay in the bed. He was a solid member of the VFW in Yuma and was known to pull a cork every now and then. Buddy was a member of the sheriff's posse search and rescue, and he rode in almost every parade in the town of Yuma. Seemed to be all right money-wise. He had sold his business down on Main Street in Yuma and retired from working every day. I was told that business was the Imperial Hardware Store, a staple business in Yuma for many a year.

It was there in Yuma, that I was set to ride saddle bronc. It was the late afternoon on this February day. The year would have been 1962, I was 15 years old at the time, and it was the Yuma Silver Spur Rodeo. My brother Billy was entered in the timed roping event and looked to do well with Duke his roping horse.

I had drawn a Cinnamon colored mare to ride for my outing which was a color called Grullo by horse people. I kept thinking about the hours I had spent up to this day on a 55 Gallon drum with my rig strapped to it, practicing moving my legs and feet in rhythm to spur the imaginary horse on. Hours working the hand grip strengthener so I could get a firm grip on the rein. Getting myself mentally ready for the ride was most of the battle in this sport. Getting better meant getting stronger both physically and mentally.

I was aboard the mare and leaning forward to get my right foot in the stirrup when she suddenly reared back, neck moving back at me, and hit me square in the nose with her neck. Lights almost went out for me and I did see stars, as blood flew from my nose and all over my face and shirt. I was stunned and lost my hat at the same time.

As I sat there for a few moments I thought the ride was over for me and that I would not be able to go on. Buddy, was suddenly at the gate and said "Hold on son, I'll get your hat." I remember saying something about not being able to do this ride, and Buddy spoke to reassure me that I could do this ride if I wanted to. "You have a chance here son, to prove your mettle. I'm sure you can get a re-ride for later, but I'll Goddamn sure guarantee you, in about 30 minutes or so your eyes are going to be dam near swollen shut and you won't be able to find your own ass. This is your time and your chance to ride this Bronc. God might forgive you if you quit, but you won't, and you never will."

Looking at Buddy I saw in him the confidence he had that I could do this. I took my hat from him, screwed it down tight on my head, put my foot in the missing stirrup, and said "Let's Do This."

I didn't consider the events up to that moment of the ride to be reason enough not to go on with what was in front of me. I came to ride and that was what I wanted to do more than wipe the blood from my nose and quit.

Buddy came up to me after my ride and said " You know I've seen a few things in my years rodeoing, but watching you do what you did right there, is mostly near the top." I thanked Buddy for pushing me onward with the ride and told him for sure I would never forget him. He said " Dam Son, that's the highest praise I could ever hope for. "

Yes Sir, a lot of years have passed since that late afternoon day in February. I have to admit I was ready to quit that horse right then and there with a broken nose as my trophy. Buddy showed me where to find the courage to go on in the face of adversity. His words ring true today just as they did 60 years ago in that dirt arena with blood flowing down my neck in old Yuma. "God might forgive you if you quit, but you won't and you never will." The lessons for our learning are not always easy to find in this world. When one of them comes at you, even at the expense of getting a broken nose, grab it and hold on to it as if your life depends on it, cause it does.

Regarding the ride, I made on that Cinnamon colored mare, with blood flowing from my nose. I did the best I could and scored the best I could.

That's what life is really all about after all. Just do the best you can, with what you have.

My story moves ahead in time to 1982. I was made aware of the passing of Buddy in Yuma. I had stayed in touch with Buddy over the years and we had developed a real friendship. I made it a point to be at the funeral for him to pay my respects for what he had done for me. I met with the family members of Buddy the day before the funeral, and after telling his family about my rodeo encounter with Buddy, they wanted me to tell the story of the Cinnamon mare at the rodeo in 1962. I would like to think the retelling of that event was well accepted by the folks in attendance at the funeral. I know for a fact people come into and out of our lives for reasons we can not understand at the time. Using Buddy's own words, about the choices we make along the way "God might forgive you if you quit, but you won't, and you never will." Getting to know Buddy, and having him in my life was one of the most amazing friendships I have ever known. To say it like he would " it was mostly at the top."

KOFA Days

My high school was KOFA High School which stood for King of Arizona named after a famous mine there in Yuma County Arizona. I went there from 1960 to 1964 and did get my high school diploma from that school.

Turned out at the time of graduation I was in the hospital recovering from an injury and could not attend the graduation ceremony. The injury occurred involving a car, a canal bank road, and beer. How I did not die as a result of the foolishness is a wonder to this very day. Thank You, Lord.

I always took my lunch to school back in those high school days. A sandwich and a cup of coffee suited me just fine. I always sat at a table out in the open area between the buildings and didn't really care to be inside the cafeteria. I really do not remember anyone ever sitting with me at that table on any given day. I knew a few of the kids that I went to school with over the years. Hard not to know people you see almost every day, and sit with in class. I just liked being alone most of the time and especially when eating my sandwich and drinking my coffee. Buying food at school was not my thing and I never wanted more than I brought with me. Skinny kid in those days and always was.

Then one day a girl sat down at the same table and after a few moments asked me if I was new in school. I had gone to school with this girl for about 5 years or more and had seen her every day for that period of time

but I guessed she had not seen me. I told her I was new but that I would only be there for a short while and then gone to another school. She never asked more of me and that was the first and last time we ever spoke.

I felt like I lived in a bubble for the years that I went to school in Yuma.

It was not hard for me to do that. Had a teacher sit at the table with me once and we never spoke. I must have been invisible to all those people and that is just the way I liked it. Never considered myself to be different from all the other kids, just not sociable when I was around them.

Sports at school was never a strong desire for me. Tried track once and found I was not a fast runner. When events in track conflicted with my rodeo adventures I was absent from track. The result of that was the coach asking me to not be part of the team anymore. I said that would suit me just fine. He seemed concerned that I was not upset and wanted to know why. I told him I just didn't care about the sport and I would just as soon not be part of it. It didn't count toward my grades anyway and it was not enjoyable for me. Four years at that school and no sporting event to show for it on a letterman's sweater. My mother insisted I purchase a class ring from Kofa High and I did. Never wore the ring and still have it. Maybe that's why I still have it because I didn't want it in the first place.

I walked to school until in my Junior year at Kofa when I finally got my hot rod running and licensed and insured. 1940 Chevrolet Coupe with an altered engine and transmission. It was quick but it was not fast, if you know what I mean. An eye-catcher for sure in and around old Yuma town.

Had it painted Sierra Gold, and put reverse chrome wheels on it. Sure was a hoot to drive to and from school. Some days even with the car I would walk to save gas for Friday Night. Friday Night was time for the drive-in movies and of course time for a coke and burger down at the Tip Top Drive Inn. I didn't go that often cause I didn't have a girl to take with me and going solo was not looked upon as being cool. Of course, there were a lot of girls hanging out down at the Tip Top but it was the same old story of

who are you and where do you go to school. That's the part of being a no body that seemed to fit me in and out of school but not at the Tip Top.

Besides Friday nights were roping nights and Saturdays were riding days.

Didn't leave a lot of time for Romeo to make a connection, and it sure wasn't going to be in school.

To find someone else, it has been said, you first have to find yourself. I took it slow in the self-development department of my life. I knew I wanted to be part of the bigger picture of life around me, but how to get there was a puzzle. My big brother was quick to point out that my interest in horses could be put to good use if I was willing. I was willing and it turned out to be the door to the world outside myself that I never dreamed it would be.

I found myself living a double life. One life involved going to school and interacting as little as possible with kids my age, The other life was one of being around equine and doing the things I wanted to do more than anything else. It was easy for me to do and I really did not see any conflict with being two people in one person. I felt like I was in standby mode when I was in school, and came to life when I was with Billy and going to Rodeo's. School had no hold on me and I was not the least bit interested in being there. I did what I had to do to keep up my grades, but nothing more.

Some years later I met people who said they went to Kofa High also and they all said they did not remember me going to that school. When asked about teachers and other kids I would not have any positive response cause I just did not remember any of them. I still have my senior year class book showing all the kids and teachers. I have looked at it several times over the years and still do not remember faces and places. I would guess that my wanting to remain anonymous as a student worked well for me.

I just didn't care to be involved with those people and it really has not changed to this day. The house I lived in growing up was my home, not the schools, not the city, and not the people.

Nacona
10 Years Old

"Ahalani Cha" Comanche . Live in Harmony with the Sun.

I knew a Comanche Man in Yuma when I was but a boy, his name was Nacona He was an older American Indian man, and worked for the horsemen's association Nacona was a Horse Grader and Certifier of horses and other livestock. His qualifications for determining Age, Breed, Training, and Background of horses were well recognized throughout the western states. His skills earned him a nice living and he traveled a lot, to be where horses were bought, sold, and auctioned.

I knew the man that he was when I was about 10 years old. His name Nacona means. One who wanders. He called me Koda which means Friend. At the time I came to know him, he had a bad tooth that was bothering him. My brother Billy took him to Algodones, Mexico, and got him fixed up with a very good and inexpensive dentist. He was in my life with horses for about a year. During the time I knew Nacona I learned many things about horses and about life as a Human Being as he would refer to us. I had never known a person as gentile and deliberate of deed and spoken word as Nacona. I have never met anyone like him in my lifetime.

When Nacona left Yuma, he told me I will never see him again in this life. He knew what I did not know about gain and loss in this life. He told me I would have many adventures and I should never lose sight of the center line of my time here as a human being. He said the four winds and the great spirit will guide me if I allow it. His vision for my life was that I would become a dream seeker. He said "Ahalani Cha " and called me Koda. A boy, an older Comanche man, and Horses, the setting for a friendship still remembered. I have often wondered how we became friends and still marvel at it.

Do I miss those people and horses? Not at all, they are with me always. They are the fence posts and pastures of all my memories. They are hard and soft leather, alive as ever in my mind. Yuma to me is all dreams of a life lived so long ago and so far away. They are the dreams I want to share with you. Will I ever be able to do that? Knowing my life as lived so far, I'd have to say No.

What we want and what we get, we soon lose. Such is the way of the world. Mostly we don't get what we want and have to settle for what we are allowed to have. More fortunate than most I got to live with the most incredible person I have ever met, her name was Georgia. She too has become a Dream. Georgia, like Nacona, knew I would never see her again once she was gone from this world. She knew that in Heaven we will not have need of past lives in this world and they will be of no importance. In this life, we think that reconnecting in the after life is so important and in the end, it is not. I guess I am one of the many who feel seeing our loved ones in heaven is so damned important. I sure would love to see her again but what will be and what I want are always very different.

Thinking as I sit here about my Old Friend Nacona. The four winds have indeed brought me to this place I am at in this life. The great spirit has led me through it all and I owe him all that I have and all that I am. Ahalani Cha - Live in harmony with the Sun - Koda - Friend. I have dreams for a lifetime.

Rough Stock

After two years of riding rough stock, I was getting better at the game. Moved from bareback to saddle bronc with ease, not giving either one my all. Felt good standing in the dirt outside the pens that held the horses for the rodeo. The rodeo would start the following day and I was anxious to get going once again. Billy, my older brother, was there as well to see the size of the calves he would be roping in his tie down event. Billy was also a member of the J.C.'s (Junior Chamber of Commerce) mounted posse and seemed like he knew everyone. Successful as a Calf Roper right there in Yuma, people knew who he was. They didn't know me as his little brother but I hoped one day that would change as I got better at riding.

It was a Tuesday, January 31, and a school day but I didn't give a rip about school when the rodeo came to town. I was meant to rodeo and school just got in my way. The Silver Spur Rodeo in Yuma, Arizona was a big event for contestants from all over the southwest. This was 1962 and the rodeo was to run for four days ending on Saturday, July 4th. I wasn't in the riding for money but the chance to win a buckle was paramount on my mind. Little Britches events were popular in those days and there were a lot of boys from around the area that entered to try their hands at riding. I was just another one of those kids with big dreams about being a professional bronc rider one day. For now, I was listed in the junior class of the boys strictly by my age, which was 14 at the time. There was only one other boy from my school that was a contestant, and we agreed not to discuss our riding with anyone, in school or out of school. I was a nobody at rodeo events and wanted to keep it that way. Even had the announcers at these events call my name as Little Brother so as not to call attention to who I was.

I Had a crush on a high school girl I had been going to school with since grade school. Prettiest girl I had ever seen, but I never talked to her. She didn't know who I was and I planned to keep it that way. I had a fear she would attend the rodeo and see me for who I was and know me from school. Just a shy boy not familiar with girls or their ways, I just wanted to remain a nobody to everyone. Billy said I was crazy not to talk to her, or get to know her. He said she might be a real stinker and then I could forget her and move on. I knew he was right, I just couldn't do what he said I should do. Turns out I never did speak to her, and for sure she never did know me.

Billy had a girlfriend named Sandy, she was the daughter of a minister there in Yuma. Pretty girl and loved Billy for sure. He said he will marry her soon, but for now, they are just close friends. Sandy doesn't like Billy doing his roping at rodeo events, she says he could get hurt really bad.

I said, "Heck yah, ain't it great?" She did not see the humor in that remark.

9:00 am and time for me to go to school. I'll be marked late but I don't care. I will have to go to the school office to get a pass to allow me into my assigned class at that hour. They will no doubt ask why I am late arriving at school and I will have to tell them something. I planned to tell them I was attending the morning milking down at the Henry Plyeman Dairy and lost track of time. Like they really care anyway, they don't. My first event for riding is tomorrow, at 4:00 pm and I'd be done with school for the day. The events after that were later in the day and I'd be fine and not miss any school time. Mom would insist on that, and Dad was her enforcer.

Before we left the arena Billy and I went to the main office for the rodeo and I got to see the buckles on display. I was mesmerized by the Silver and Gold Yuma Silver Spur Rodeo Buckles. Billy has more than a couple from this rodeo and I sure hope to get one for my event. Man, there said they had several entries for Bareback Riding but very few for Saddle Bronc.

I had done Saddle Bronc mostly so didn't see any reason to switch over to Bareback. I got my riding numbers for the back of my shirt and Billy got his. We were all set for the next day's opening and I was excited about it as always. Just then a girl walked into the office to get signed up for Barrel Racing. She was very pretty and we did make eye contact. Said her name was Jen short for Jennifer, and looking at my numbers for riding wished me luck tomorrow. I said the same to her and said I'd sure watch for her. Billy gave me space and didn't hurry me at all while I spoke to the girl. Said she goes to Yuma High and I told her I was at Kofa, and my name was Bruce. I asked if I could see her to do something away from the rodeo, and she said I sure could. I then walked out of the office and looked at Billy, who was all smiles. Maybe I could talk to girls after all. Billy, said do you have her phone number? I went back to the office and got the number. Starting to get the hang of it all. Always told Billy, riding rank horses is easier than talking to girls. He told me it would not always be like that. One day I would lose interest in riding horses at rodeos but I would never lose interest in girls. I hoped to be able to make these predictions for myself soon.

The following day the rodeo began and I just couldn't wait to get there. School for me was over at 3:00 pm and Billy was in the parking lot waiting for me. We got over to the rodeo grounds found a parking spot for the truck and trailer. Billy wished me luck and went to attend to Duke his roping horse. I headed over to the riders gathering point and got checked in. I was assigned my horse for the ride and given my chute number. This was the time I would get all flushed and excited knowing what was coming but kept my composure and watched as the other riders dealt with the same feelings. I didn't see that other boy from my school that was to ride at the rodeo, but he could be running late or got the butterflies so bad he decided not to ride.

My time came quickly and I got ready for the ride. Hardest part of getting set was to zip up and tighten my chaps. Nothing fancy in what I wore they were old and hand-me-down leathers with silver conchos down both legs, but they worked and made me look more like a pro than I would ever be. They were Bullhide and stiff making me walk funny with them on, but they saved my bacon many times over the years that I wore them. Had drilled a hole through the center of two quarters and mounted them on my old spurs as rowels cause the originals went missing somewhere. I was indeed a 50-cent cowboy. The girl Jen, I met the day before came up to me as I was buttoning up and said to be careful out there and said she just wanted me to know she was there for me. I must have turned red as a tomato cause she laughed and then walked away. A girl was routing for me. A very pretty girl was routing for me. I sure didn't expect that before my first ride.

Riding in front of my home town crowd didn't occur to me as anything different than what I had already done in other little towns around the state. They didn't know me and I didn't know them. My first horse was a dark sorrel mare named "StarLite" and as I slid down on her she remained very steady and calm. The moment had come for me to show what I could do.

I pulled my hat down tight, firmed my grip on the rein, gave the nod to make it happen, the chute opened, and I spurred out as best I could. From that point on I was having a ball doing what I knew I was meant to be doing. I heard the buzzer and looked for the pickup rider, realizing I had made the 8 count and the ride was a success. As I walked out of the arena I had one thought on my mind, I wanted to see Jen again. She was there at the back of the chutes and I could not believe how pretty she was. Such a sweet girl and she was more than ready to hug me for the ride. I thought my heart would burst with pride at the full ride and now at the girl in my arms. Billy, was there as well and said I did good. He was referring to my ride as well as the girl I was holding in front of everyone. Billy was happy and timed well in his event and was in the run for money.

Saddle Bronc Riding

*Following are the rules and regulations for the event of saddle bronc riding as provided by District 4 High School Rodeo

As in the other riding events, the two judges on either side of the chute each score the horse and rider on 1 to 25-point spreads, for a total possible 50 points for horse and 50 points for rider giving a combined total of 100 points for a perfect ride.

The saddle bronc, like the bareback horse, is rated on how high he kicks, the strength and force of his bucking action, his reverses in direction, and for rolling and twisting action. For the control looked for by the judges, the saddle bronc rider's spurring action must be exquisitely timed to the horse's bucking rhythm. The more the rider turns out his toes, the more his spurs will drag in contact with the horse. Length of stroke from neck rearward to the back of the saddle also increases the rider's score. Riding rein and hand must be on same side.

To qualify, rider must have spurs over the break of the shoulders and touching horse when the horse's front feet hit the ground first jump out of the chute. Ride for eight seconds. A rider will be disqualified for being bucked off; changing hands on the rein; losing stirrup; or touching the animal, saddle or rein with the free hand.

In the classic event of rodeo, an outstanding saddle bronc rider is a beautifully choreographed dance of man and wild horse pitted spirit to spirit in intense poetry in motion.

The Pattern.

In barrel racing, three barrels are set up in a triangular pattern— measurements between barrels and how close the barrels are to the fence are set at the discretion of the event producer and/or sanctioning body. Each rider must turn each barrel while navigating the cloverleaf pattern as fast as he or she can. Riders may choose to approach the right or left barrel first. The right barrel is most-commonly selected as the first barrel, requiring one right-hand turn and two left-hand turns.

The Times.

In barrel racing, the fastest time wins. However, in a divisional race with a 4D format, riders can win money by placing in a division. This means that the 1D is the fastest time of the race, the 2D is the winning time plus half a second, the 3D is the winning time plus one second and the 4D is the winning time plus two seconds.

The Penalties.

If a horse and rider team goes off pattern, this results in a no time. Knocking a barrel is a plus-five-second penalty at rodeos or results in a no time at a divisional race. Riders are allowed to touch the barrel and if it doesn't fall completely over, a penalty can be avoided.

TIE DOWN ROPING RULES

Tie down roping shall be timed in one hundreds (7.89). Rope may be dallied or tied hard and fast. The contestant must rope the calf, dismount, go down rope and throw the calf by hand, cross, and tie any 3 feet. To qualify as a legal tie, there shall be at least one (1) wrap around all three legs with a three-bone cross and half hitch (hooey). If the calf is down when the roper reaches it, the calf must be let up to a vertical position with feet dangling underneath and re-thrown by hand. If the roper's hand is on the calf when the calf falls, the calf is considered thrown by hand. The rope must be on the calf when the roper touches the calf. If you are unable to get the calf up, there will be a 1.5-second penalty. The calf must remain crossed and tied for 6 seconds. Time begins when the roper rides up And provides slack in the rope. After calling for time, the roper may not touch the rope, tie, or calf until the judge has completed his examination. The field judge will use a stopwatch timing six (6) seconds which will begin when the roper rides forward providing slack in the rope. In the event a rope comes off the calf while competing, the six (6) second time period will begin after the roper calls for time and clears the calf. THE FLAG JUDGE MUST WATCH CALF during the 6-second period and will stopwatch if the calf kicks free, using the time on the watch to determine whether the calf was tied long enough to qualify.

A contestant may have someone push their calf out of the chute. No pusher will be allowed to follow the calf out of the chute in the act of tailing the calf. This will incur an immediate disqualification.

If the barrier jerks the calf around and knocks the calf down, a re-run will be awarded. Roper will receive the first extra calf, if extras are available, or will use the miss-draw procedure.

No re-run for faking a judge into giving an early flag.

In any case, if a permanent fixture fouls the roper, no re-run will be awarded.

Roper will be disqualified by removing the rope from the calf after signaling for time until the tie has been ruled on by the field Judge.

Neck ropes must be tied with string or rubber bands. No metal snaps or hardware shall be used on neck rope in the timed events.

If in the opinion of the barrier judge, the contestant is fouled (including any penalties) by the barrier, the roper shall get calf over, provided the contestant declares himself immediately by pulling up the horse. Hitting a stationary object such as a fence, pole, chute, etc. is the roper's responsibility. No re-runs.

If a roper intentionally abuses a calf, the roper will be disqualified and fined a minimum of $100.00 and up to $250.00.

When the barrier is stretched and the animal is standing, the contestant has a 45-second time limit to call for stock. After 45 seconds the animal will be released and the contestant receives a no time.

There will be no ground money. In case of only one qualified run, the qualifying contestant will receive all money in that event. Points will count for all money paid. If no qualified runs, the stock contractor will receive all the money.

Contestants will be fined $75.00 for the jerk-down infraction. "Jerk down" will be defined as over backward, with the calf landing on his back or head with all four feet in the air.

All judges' decisions will be final.

Wasn't long after my ride I got to see Jen compete in the Barrel Racing and she did exceptionally well on her run. It was then my turn to return the hug and she was more than willing to accept my congratulations on her accomplishment in her age group. I offered to buy her a burger at the concession stand and she accepted. My first date with a real girl, was at a rodeo. I am liking this part of my day the best of all. I had a Ten Dollar Bill and that was a lot of money back in that day. I was at a rodeo, I was with a girl, and I was on top of the world in little old Yuma.

Gas Pump

A Winter night in Yuma. 1962 according to my memory of the time. I'm standing in a vacant lot beside the Blakely's Gas Station at 28th Street and 4th Avenue. It's 2:30 am on a Sunday morning, just after Thanksgiving. Got my warmest jacket on 'cause it's cold and rainy.

Standing there smelling the wet sand in the lot, thinking about where I was and what I was going to do with my life. Didn't make much money pumping gas. Sure wasn't thinking about a career doing this for much longer. Had to finish High School before doing much in the way of planning my great move to become rich. Nothing going on at the station and I was close enough to get to any cars that pulled in for gas.

Gas was selling for 29 cents a gallon for regular. Price went up and down, but never more than a couple cents over the course of that year. Still did a full service at the pump in those days. Check under the hood and gauge the tires, after asking what they keep for pressure. If they didn't know then it was up to me. Every now and then a car would pull in that I was not familiar with and I'd have to ask where the gas cap was. I was just a kid so they pretty much expected that.

Kept a pot of coffee on for the Police and occasional Sheriff's Deputy. Sometimes both at the same time. Nights were mostly slow and I figured out that's why I had the job. Never made more than about $50.00 a week, but it kept gas in my motorcycle and kept me mobile around town, and out of trouble. Entry fees at the rodeos kept me mostly out of money, and for some reason, I thought spending my money like that was important at the time.

Next door to the station was Joe Hunt's Steak House and Lounge. Many a drunk came out of that place and drove off down the street. Drunk driving was a bad thing even back then, but everybody knew everybody and the cops seemed to know everyone also. Never saw many people getting stopped in the middle of the night for anything, except when they had an accident.

Cold and rainy night on that early Sunday morning. My feet were getting cold standing in that wet sand, so I shuffled over to the office to warm up a bit. The cleaning crew was just walking out of Joe Hunt's and heading for home. The night bartender was also leaving and as usual, he was drunk.

Dropped his keys at least 5 or 6 times before he got to his car. Had to hold on to the railing around the walkway just to get that far. Finally got his door open and seated himself just before falling down and sat for the longest time figuring out what to do next. Then his car started and it ran for several minutes before moving in reverse for a distance. Sat again for several minutes and then went into forward gear. Jumped over two parking blocks and then over the curb out onto 4th Avenue and headed north across the center of the road and then back again to the proper side. Yes, I knew him. Mr. Hannes was a deacon at the First Baptist Church down at 4th Avenue and Third Street. Wore the same gray suit to church every Sunday for as long as I can remember. Member of the Joe Hunt's Bowling League on Tuesday nights and active in the local El Zaribah Shrine. Volunteer down at the Yuma Food Bank. Always spoke kindly to my Mom at church and was nice to my father whenever my father would go to church with Mom and me.

This station and the Chevron Station at 1st Street and 4th Avenue were the only two stations that stayed open all night in Yuma in 1962. I knew Micky, the kid that ran that Chevron station. He was a good friend of mine and we rode around town on our motorbikes together. Mickey was sure he was going to own his station one day, 'cause he loved doing this kind of work. We were the same age and went to school together up until we finished the eighth grade, that's when Micky quit going to school. Said he didn't like it and it was too hard for him. Micky always wore jeans rolled up at the ankle. White socks and black penny loafers were his stock and trade. White t-shirt with a pack of Lucky's rolled up in the shirt sleeve. His hair was a dark brown and always greased back with the ends curly. I often wondered how he got so smart as to know he wasn't so smart. I hadn't figured out if I was smart or not and didn't give it much thought. I guess I had formulated a theory that the older one gets the smarter one becomes. That happens with or without schooling in my theory. So, as I figured it, I'd have to wait a while to see if I was smart or not. Kind of took all the guesswork away. Getting older and going to school was supposed to make me ahead of Micky by a long shot. Micky's father was the manager at the Blakely's Station where I worked. He told me once to keep a close eye on Micky, as he had it on good authority that Micky wasn't right in the head in a lot of ways. I kept that little bit of information between me and Micky's dad. Never gave it much thought until I was a good deal older and a lot more savvy to the ways of people.

Had the work bays all closed up but without heat, it was still cold in them. Decided to change the oil in my motorcycle. So I did that and topped off my gas tank at the pump. Paid for the gas I took and made sure I wrote it down for the boss. I had already cleaned the bathrooms and hosed down the drive from the mud that had been tracked in. Restocked all the wiper blades and oil cans in the rack.

Sitting in the office staring out the window I thought about all the places I was going to go when I got older and smarter. As young as I was then I had already figured out that a person can go a long ways on nothing, but when you get where you're going you still have nothing.

I finished high school and during my senior year, I lost track of Micky. I had quit working the night shift at the gas station for quite a while. He and I were no longer close as we once were and I had a girlfriend and horses to keep me busy. Didn't need the bike anymore and had moved on to a car. Went through my phase of Rodeo every time I could. Next thing you know I'm enlisted in the US Navy and headed for places unknown. I was making my big escape from little Yuma.

Years went by and after the Navy, I became a Tempe Police Officer and was fortunate enough to become a Motorcycle Officer. Back to riding a motorcycle just like when I was hanging around Micky back in Yuma. Seems some things come full circle if we pay attention. My training for the job was at the Los Angeles Police Motorcycle Training Academy, and it was the toughest thing I had ever done. Needless to say, when I came back to Tempe I could ride that bike better than 99.9% of the motoring public.

Then came word that Micky had been killed in an accident in north Phoenix. I received the address of his parents and went to see them when I got off work. Everyone that was there was friends we had shared over the years that we were best pals, and they were glad to see me and we talked a lot about Micky and the years that had passed since we were together. The accident was tragic and Micky was killed outright and did not suffer prolonged pain and injury. Seems Micky was true to his word and stayed in the gas station business all these years. I figured it had been 7 or 8 years since I had seen him. He was the manager at the Roadrunner Truck Stop in Phoenix and was very successful at his work. He was not married but had a girlfriend and I got to meet her. During my visit with the family, I spoke with Micky's father alone and recounted to him the conversation we had many years before. I told him he had said that Micky was not right in the head in a lot of ways, and wondered about that. He told me Micky was stuck mentally at about the age of 16, and never seemed to grow beyond that. In a lot of ways, it was always fun to be around him as he was young of heart and mind. But Micky did not understand that growing up and getting older was needed in this world, and along with those things came responsibility which he was lacking. He told his father all the time that he missed being with me and the fun we had. While still in Yuma, he would go over to my folks' house to read the mail I sent them from wherever I was in the Navy. Mom often told me he was still like the kid we were at the time we were together.

I left the house of Micky's parents that day feeling really down. I had always felt that Micky was smart for knowing his own shortcomings. I then realized that I was smart to have moved away from Yuma and to have started a new life at least twice since being with Micky. I have never seen Micky's parents or family since that day. I had been hurt way down deep inside by Micky's death and didn't want anymore. The doorway to the past for me was closed on that part of my life. It seems there are many doors to open for us and a whole lot of them to close.

I have never had any preconceived notions about what my life was going to be, or what I was going to become other than older and maybe a bit wiser because of it. Riding a motorcycle, working at a gas station, knowing old man Hannes the drunk, and still wondering about life seemed to be what I was meant to do. Leaving Yuma, and the life I knew then was also part of my path in this world.

Micky the 16-year-old I knew way back then was part of my life and always will be. I miss being 16 years old and I miss Micky. What I'm saying is that I really do miss Yuma, and those days of innocence and adventure. I miss them a lot.

Down on the Corner

On the corner of 8th Street and Avenue C was a small mom-and-pop food store the name of which I do not recall. Was a Chinese family that ran the place and I used to stop in there to buy stuff from time to time. Mostly sodas and smokes and sometimes beer, see he didn't care about my age.

I remember the beer he carried that was cheap, it was Regal Pale Beer and he charged sixty-nine cents a six-pack for it.

On the one Television Station, we had back home was a TV show on Saturday Nights called the Harry Owens Show, and it was broadcast from The Royal Hawaiian Village in Honolulu, Hawaii. It was all Hawaiian Music and had stars like Hilo Hattie and Ponce Ponce which were very entertaining to folks living on the desert in southern Arizona. I was told that the Host of the TV show, Harry Owens, was a very famous songwriter and band leader of the Hawaiian Music that he and his Orchestra played.

Since my father controlled the TV set in our home, he decided what we watched if anything, and on Saturday Night, if he was home, it was the Harry Owens Show. My father being a Fireman for the city was gone 24 hours and then home 24 hours leaving the TV set to whoever had the desire to watch it every other day without his control.

Well as it turns out the Harry Owens Show was sponsored by Regal Pale Beer. So there you have the connection to the Chinaman's store down on 8th Street and Avenue C and the fact that Regal Pale Beer was sixty-nine cents a six-pack. I was driving a car at the time and I was interested in buying beer so I must a been at least 16 years old, more than likely 17 years old.

At 17 years old I was a Senior in high school, very much into my horse riding adventures with my brother, and not at all chasing after girls. I don't recall any girls having an interest in me, and I pretty much was on my own during that time.

Never was interested in school sports or any other activities like Drama, or Band, and such. Didn't want to be in school during those high school years, it had no appeal to me whatsoever. Little did I know that a whole bunch of years later I would try to remember back to those high school years and search my memory for people and places. Not having had any impact on me those years are pretty much blank and rightfully so.

Turned 18 in December 1964, and in January 1965 found me in boot camp with the US Navy, in San Diego, California. The Navy brought about many changes in my way of thinking about life. I went to many schools to be taught about Electronics and how it was to be part of my life in Naval Aviation. In August of 1966, I found myself at my assigned duty station for the remainder of my four-year hitch. It was Barbers Point Naval Air Station, Oahu, Hawaii.

A boy in Yuma watching a Hawaiian Music Show, sponsored by Regal Pale Beer which as I learned later was brewed in San Fransisco from 1958 to 1962. Seems the brewery was very prolific in brewing the Regal Pale product as supplies at very low prices were available years after they quit making the stuff. How would I have known in Yuma I was drinking not only cheap beer made by a defunct brewery but that the beer itself was old by a number of years? It occurs to me now that the Chinaman at the corner store would sell that old beer to anyone just to get rid of it. The Chinaman's daughter who worked in the store where I bought the beer also sold the beer to me and she knew me and my age very well as we went to high school together. I always thought she was very pretty and she always smiled at me when I came to the store. She always had time for me in school and sat with me often during lunch break. I asked her to go to a picture show with me and she always said No, as her father would not approve. Her father was related to Kinyon Hong, who owned the Central Market at 3rd Street and 4th Avenue. The biggest grocery store in the town of Yuma and the most successful store of any kind in the town. The girl's name was Mae Lee, and she was as I said, very pretty.

The irony does not stop there of course, because it did not take me long to realize that in Hawaii they had a beer "Primo" that was the equal to Regal Pale Beer in both cost and in taste. Not only was it cheap to buy it was cheap to drink by which I mean it was not only at the low end of the beer scale of good brews it was to my inexperienced pallet the worst beer ever. In 1966 the Primo Brand Beer of Hawaii was bought by the Schlitz Brewing Company but still made in Hawaii.

So here we have the tale of the boy from Yuma, Arizona, the trail of the cheap beer saga, and Hawaiian Music. Hawaiian Music on the TV, cheap beer at the corner store, ending up in Hawaii with the Navy, and finding Hawaiian Music again, and cheap beer to go with it. When I got the time away from the Navy Base, I found myself down at the Royal Hawaiian in Honolulu listening to real Hawaiian Music being played by real Hawaiian Musicians. Curiously they did not offer Primo Beer on their beverage menu. I thought that was odd being that it was a locally brewed beer there in Hawaii. This whole thing started back in Yuma at the Chinaman's Store down on the corner in the valley. I Hope Mae Lee is doing well with her life.

The Wind

5 or 6 Years Old

Inside my home as a child I would look out the window to see the wind move the sand. Outside the wind would blind the on looker but behind glass I could watch the magic. The wind would take the sand and throw it against anything and everything. The sand didn't seem to care as it knew no amount of anger the wind could send would hurt it.

From my safe vantage point, I could watch the dance of the sand and the wind. I knew it would never change and I could come back again and again to see the rivals moving in tune with nature's song. The sand would pile up on our front porch and then be moved to another location as if the wind couldn't make up its mind where it wanted it. The wind didn't seem to mind me watching and the sand just moved on its way without a care about the boy in the window. I have often thought about the Wind and the Sand as my life moves as it does. The similarities are amazing to think of. I truly feel like Sand being blown about by the Wind as I move from place to place and person to person. I don't fear the Wind it is the force that drives us, just like it drives the sand. I don't know where I will be taken next but it's all in a plan I will one day know. I have always believed that when I die I will become the Wind and go wherever I want to go.

When leaving Yuma go straight East on 32nd Street till you get to Araby Road. Gas up there then stand in the parking lot and let the wind whisper to you that he hopes you have a safe journey. I have known the wind all my life and I have always paid attention to him. He brings dreams to those that would listen, and goodbyes when the time is due. Every time I visit Yuma, I greet him and he always welcomes me home. Hot or Cold the season does little to change the temper of the wind. It never rests in that part of the world and even in the dead of night it stirs to be noticed and appreciated. Sometimes the wind brings Sage to the senses, other times the wind brings the smell of Greasewood or Mesquite. The wind can howl almost anywhere it wants, and it does so to remind us he is there. Outside in the distance, the wind gathers up the sand and carries it to wherever you are and makes it part of your world. The wind is the ladle in the stirring pot of time and moves the sand and rain on the desert. In all the years I have known the wind he has always been my friend. The Mexicans call the wind "El Viento". They say "Siempre hay algo en el Viento" There is always something in the wind. There always was something in the wind in my hometown. The heat, the cold, the smells of the desert, or the smells of someone cooking something. My mother would make Lie Soap to clean my father's clothes of grease and oil products as he was an auto mechanic. That smell is so vivid even to this day in my memory.

Everything moves on the wind and everything moves with the wind. As a paperboy in Yuma, I would ride my bike with and against the wind. It was a time of getting up early in the morning on Saturday and Sunday to get going with my paper route. The papers were delivered to my pickup point between 4:30 and 5:00 am and I was always there to get them. I used a friend's carport at that location to roll or fold the papers depending on how thick they were. Sunday always got folded and I had two canvas bags mounted on my handlebars to accommodate the load which was substantial. Some days the rain was heavy in the early morning and I had to bag each paper and put it on the doorstep of the homes. The wind always helped me in my assigned rounds which I appreciated. Alone in the dark doing my paper route was where I loved to be. Just me and my friend the wind.

Rain on the Desert

35 Years Old

Standing alone at a roadside rest stop on Interstate 8 halfway between Gila Bend and Yuma, Arizona, it occurred to me, I am where I belong in this world. At this age in my life living on the Great Southwest Desert is life as no other life anywhere on this planet I stood there watching the rain from the distant hills cover the ground, and I knew it was all well with me and my God. The clouds in my sight were so low and thick I could actually reach out and touch them and feel his shroud against my skin.

The Sun was still up there somewhere but not visible at all as the rain clouds took center stage. The smell of the rain on the desert mixed with a hint of sage and greasewood is so crisp and clean that nothing else can take its place. It puts Thanksgiving Turkey fresh out of the oven and Mom's Hot Apple Pie in the back seat of all things good and meaningful in this world. This place in this space and time, is the closest I will ever come to heaven here on earth. I know I must leave and move on down the highway to my destination but I am torn between staying and going.

Eventually, I will have to go for I know this place and this feeling will go with me and I can recall it anytime I want to. This calm and peaceful feeling stays just beyond my senses and I can go there when I need to get away. There I find that special magical destination in my heart and soul that gives me tranquility and the reason for my sanity if there is any in this crazy world.

Saying Goodbye to Gramps

19 Years Old

I remember calling home one afternoon while away in the Navy to check up on Mom and Dad, the year was 1966. Grandpa was living with them at that time and if possible I wanted to talk to him too. Mom said everything was fine and that it sure was good to hear from me. Spoke to her for a bit and she told me Grandpa was a real handful to deal with lately. I asked if Grandpa was able to come to the phone. She said she would go get him and I waited for him. Grandpa sounded different to me as he spoke. He seemed a bit distant in his speech but I could still hear him.

" Hi Gramps, this is Bruce, how ya doing ? "

" A lot better now that I'm talking to you. Listen to what I have to say and don't speak. I'm getting ready to go on a long trip. A trip I been planning to take for some time. I'm going alone and I'll be gone a long long time. I'm tired more than ever and getting up every morning out of bed just ain't worth it. "

"Gramps, are you going to visit relatives?"

"You bet I am, a whole bunch of 'em that I ain't seen now for many a year. We have had a lot of fun together since I got to know ya. Never knew you were coming along when you did. Times were good and watching you grow was fun for me. That time has come to an end, you need to go on and live your life. I just wanted you to know that I love you and that we really had some great times together along the way. Most of all I wanted you to know that I consider you to be my best friend. Goodbye boy, take care of yourself. I'll see you again one day. "

Mom came back on the phone and asked if I had a nice talk with Grandpa, she didn't hear any of the conversation at all. I remember to this day the way Grandpa talked and the clearness of his voice.

I had gone from child to adult some time ago but I had left the door open along my journey for fear of losing those wonderful times forever. What I did not realize was that I was still passing from childhood to adulthood and that Grandpa was going to make that journey permanent by closing the door on my childhood.

It was two days later that I got word Grandpa was in the hospital and not doing well at all. Emergency leave was granted and I caught a flight home to see him if I could before he got worse or heaven forbid died.

I got home in the middle of the night and went right away with Dad up to see Gramps, in my Navy Uniform. When I got there he was sleeping. I held his hand and told him I was there. After several minutes Gramps opened his eyes and looked at me. His voice was soft and easy as he said

"Hey boy, you come to see me off?"

I recalled his words as he used to chase me around the yard down home in Yuma and I said

"Where you going in such a hurry? "

"Going on my last trip boy, got all I need."

"I don't want you to go just yet. Get better and we can get on with our time together. Soon as I get back from the Navy."

"I ain't got any time left in me, boy. Been figuring for ya. I was 68 when you was born an I got to spend 20 years with you. That's a lot of learning we got done together, sure been fun."

Grandpa then gripped my hand real firm, and while looking deep into my eyes said

"Live your life full as you can, go for whatever you want, and it will be yours. Keep Jesus close to you always. Find a mate you can love with all your heart and make sure she is one you can trust with your life. Love you boy."

Gramps then closed his eyes and within minutes he was gone. The door I had talked about was closed, never to be opened again.

I attended Gramp's funeral and cried a lot. Didn't have words to say anything to anyone. That marked the end of childhood for me.

I have attended many Adult Bible Study Groups over the years, and in several of them, the question was posed "Other than Jesus, who do you want most to meet in heaven and spend time with? "Most people pick names right out of the Bible like John, or Paul, or Peter. I have never had to give that question any thought at all. I want to see my Gramps.

After the funeral, I spent some time going over the tools in the old shed where he used to putter. Everything that I could see was old, well-used, and some broken. Tools that were of importance to him, and cared for as if to be used at any moment. Blades on those that would cut were honed to perfection with a light coat of oil on them to keep them from rusting. A very large scythe stood in the corner of the shed ready as it were to give grass and weed a cut right down to the ground. All manner of woodworking tools hung and laid around the place. I would suspect that in the right hands, an entire home could be built with never a need for other tools. As I held and moved the tools I felt his hands in mine and seemed to know his touch just by the feel of the wood and metal. Old cans of varnish and paint were on shelves that I could see and the smell of them was almost overwhelming. An old cook stem pipe lay in an ashtray on the workbench. It contained the half-smoked remnants of tobacco that he used, and as I looked I saw it sitting on the top of the workbench backboard. A can of Prince Albert Smoking Tobacco, along with a small leather pouch filled with the same. The floor in the shed was dirt and the marks left there were smoothed over and over by the movements of his large boots with the laces dragging as he would shuffle along. A large man but stooped in stance from the years of hard labor that had made him that way. Old slouch hat on his bald head and thick glasses tinted green as I recall to keep the desert sun from blinding him. Always busy with one project or another in his shed. The heat of the summers in Yuma did not deter him from his work. Some task or another was always at hand and he would go about doing things at a pace that would seem to be in slow motion, but he would get one thing done and then move on to the next. As a boy, I would follow him around and wonder at his seemingly never-ending work. When I would ask a question of him he would stop and look at me for the longest time, and then either ignore me or answer with a soft-spoken voice that always gave specific detail to me so I would understand. I believe it was in him to speak in a way that was understood and not questioned by the listener, even if only five or six years old.

I had learned not to run my fingers on blades that he had laying around, no matter how old or dull they might appear. They were never dull and they certainly were sharp as a razor, if they were meant to be that way. That old man never allowed any metal with a blade to be in his shed without a proper edge being on it at all times. I remember my dad taking things that needed to be sharpened to Granddad for that reason. I have often thought he did that just to give Grandpa something to do but realized after many years of working with metal edges that something's are learned only after many trials and errors. Grandpa was an expert at metal sharpening and could do it time and time again with perfection and ease.

Then it started to rain and I felt the cool of the air on my skin as I stood in that shed and marveled at Grandpa's handy work. The rain had been carried on the wind and had followed me down the highway from the rest stop. It too was coming to pay its respects to Grandpa on his funeral day. I took comfort in that thought. I remember Grandma telling me that the rain was Angels' tears that were built up in Heaven till it couldn't hold it no more. Tears are shed because of the way we live our lives here on earth and the way we treat others. I could feel my own tears rolling down my cheeks and knew I would shed many tears in years to come for loved ones at their time of passing.

My mother told me people that who die go to heaven and we will see them again when our time comes to die. She told me they would remain just as we knew them when we get to see them again. I always appreciated Mom's words to me about that. I thought then as I think about it now, that they might indeed be the same when next we see them, but we won't be the same. We have changed and grown and aged to the point that we are not the same anymore. She told me it wouldn't matter at all. We will know them.

A House and A Home

How far back in time can you go with old memories? Today I am going back to the year 1950 in Yuma, Arizona. Standing on the corner of 3rd Street and 4th Avenue in that town. North West Corner of that intersection is Central Market Grocery Store owned by Kenyon Hong. South West corner is First Baptist Church with Pastor Robert Spearing to head the flock. Crossing over 4th Avenue at 3rd Street is Yuma County Library and Park. On 3rd Street and 5th Avenue was the Bristol Brothers Dodge, Desoto, Chrysler Dealership where my father worked as an Auto Mechanic, until he got hired by the City of Yuma, to be a City Fireman in 1952.

Up until 1953 we lived at 763 Orange Avenue and the old Adobe House is still there to this day. The house was built in 1903 and was at that time 1200 square feet in size. Two small bedrooms, one old and small bathroom with a tub on legs, no shower, one kitchen, one old fireplace, and a living room about the size of a one-car garage. The house was made of Adobe Brick about 12 to 14 inches thick and had a metal roof that made noise in the rain, if it ever did rain. Out front was a Palm Tree that was old and large, the base of which would be about 25 feet around. Had old Concrete Lamp Posts with Glass tops that looked like large flames that came together at the top in a point. I don't remember the lamps giving off a great deal of light, but it was enough to bring every bug in the neighborhood to them and great fun for the kids to play under in the early evening hours. The house remained relatively cool in the heat of summer there in Yuma. One year my father somehow got an old evaporative cooler about the size of a modern refrigerator and mounted it on a wooden stand that he built at a side window of the little house. It was most powerful and the large rotor fan would blow the air in that house so hard I could not stand in front of it. The smell of the water running through the excelsior pads was magical and wonderful. The coolness of the evaporative air created by the machine was incredible and dropped the temperature in that little house by at least 20 degrees or more.

In 1953 my father qualified for a Veterans Home loan and bought a house out on what was then called the Mesa. 824 Cactus Drive was a 1200 square foot home, 3 bedroom brick home with 1 and a half baths. The cost of the home in 1953 was $8,000 and the payments were $83.00 a month a very sizable purchase for my parents at that time. Dad was a fireman for the city and mom was a nurse for a private physician at that time. The combined income for them was enough to cover the loan, pay for water and electricity, get groceries, and put gas in the cars; that was just about it.

I spent more time at that First Baptist Church than any other place in that city, almost more time than I spent at home. Sunday morning always started with Sunday School, then Church Service, then gatherings of Deacons and Elders. Sunday night was church, Wednesday night was Prayer Meeting, and Friday night was quilting or baby blanket night. Saturdays were always about the church league baseball, touch football, or basketball. By the time I was 18 years old, I was completely churched out and I stayed that way till I turned 60. Looking back on it this very day I still hate it and always will. But I know my Jesus and he goes with me where ever I go, even if it isn't to church.

From the time I was 5 years old, I lived in that house on Cactus Drive where that house was built just down from the first Mall in the town. Seemed that all the resident owners were veterans just like my father and talk of the G.I Bill was spoken of proudly. Three small bedrooms, 1 and 1/2 baths with a carport. No landscaping of any kind but my father wanted a yard with grass and trees, so he began working on that in due cour

Dad, at that time, was a Fireman for the City of Yuma, Arizona. I don't know what his pay was but I do know that the payment on that house every month was $83.00. In 1951 costs for essentials were not high, but then living wages were not high, and it was a struggle for a family of any size to make ends meet. My mother studied to be a Nurse and got hired by a physician in town to earn money to add to the family fund. Wasn't long before the doctor retired and Mom hired on at the Yuma Hospital.

When I was 8 years old I got a job with the local newspaper to deliver papers. It didn't pay much but it was work and I figured it was only right that I contribute to helping pay the bills. Mom started a saving account for me with the bank and I put my money in every week as I earned it. Dad said it was good to know we had a nest egg to rely on if times got tough. I always thought times were tough all the years I lived in that house. Mom said later on in my life that it was day to day to make it but they just kept going and that love kept us together. The love part was so common that I guess I just didn't notice, it was like the air that we all breathed.

When I was 10 years old I went up to the local A.J. Bayless Grocery Store and asked for a job. The manager of the store said I was too young for him to hire. I asked him how old I needed to be to sweep the floor or handle a mop when needed. How old to help an old lady out to her car with groceries that she had bought as a customer at the store? How old did I need to be to help customers find the items in the store that they needed to spend their money on? He hired me right there and I began my new job as a bag boy that very afternoon. Got off in time to run my paper route and called into the Newspaper to tell them I would be leaving my job at the end of the week.

The next day I told my father about my new job at the grocery store and he asked me if the store would give us a discount on groceries as I was now an employee. I told him I would ask if they did that and if they didn't then I would ask them to do that. I started thinking that as an employee at that store, my family should buy groceries there. The thinking was if I told them I would be shopping at another store because it was cheaper they might want my business and let me get a discount as a loyal and valued customer as well as an employee. It struck me that the grocery stores in town seemed to always advertise their prices for goods on the same day of the week in the local newspaper. I started paying attention to the ads and telling people about the cheaper prices across town. Wasn't long till my suggestion about employee discounts came to be at the A.J. Bayless Store. The store where I worked started telling people whatever the lower price was as advertised across town, they would honor that price on their merchandise at Bayless. Mom got a card indicating she was a member of the store family due to my job and she was extremely happy about it. I don't recall what the discount was but it helped us out a lot for us in the daily struggles of managing money. Dad said I was getting off to a good start with understanding the value of character and the worth of the earned dollar. Those words always stayed with me through the years.

Dad added a shop behind the carport of the house to house his tools and to work on cars and trucks on the side. Along with the shop he added on a big enclosed back porch for us to use. As the years moved on, no matter where the boys of the family lived, married or single, we would all gather in that little house for Thanksgiving and Christmas. Those were the greatest times of my adult life with the people that I loved and always felt safe from the outside world in that little house that I knew as my home.

In time Mom, having outlived Dad, got to the point where she needed help with her daily living and I decided to move her to be with me in the city where I lived. I liquidated all of her stuff in the house and sold it, to use the money for her upkeep and expenses. At the time I was not concerned about keeping that house and all the memories that it held. I took the memories with me and sold the real estate for what the fair market would allow and moved on. I have always thought that the price Mom and Dad paid for that little house on the mesa in 1951 was a great deal at the time. That house was the best they could do on Dad's G.I. Bill and a real financial gamble for them with their collective income. The mortgage was for 30 years and in time the folks began to double up and then triple up on their payments and Paid off the note in 20 years. They were then setting pretty well for their future. Dad retired in 1974 and Mom the following year as they wanted to travel around the country. Home was always that little place on the mesa for them and it was always home on those special visits for me over the years, with my family and kids.

Drive-In with Spud

It was late October in sleepy little Yuma. Twilight time came at about 6:00 pm which was of interest to the people heading over to the Drive-In Theater. It was Saturday Night and I didn't have a date which was not unusual. Mostly gone off on weekends fooling with rough stock with my brother Billy in some arena somewhere. Nothing going on in that regard this particular weekend. Decided I'd go see the movie playing at the Round-Up Drive-In and took Old Spud with me, my faithful sidekick dog.

I knew he wouldn't care about the movie but he liked being with me and that was all that I needed on a lonely Saturday Night like this.

Had a 1940 Chevrolet Coupe at the time and had a Rumble Seat-mounted perfectly in the trunk. Backed into our spot with the trunk lid raised we had ourselves the perfect seat for watching the show. Having our trunk raised caused no one any blocked view as we backed in just right and it was low. The poll-mounted speaker had a long cord and hung just inside the trunk space and worked fine. We had ourselves food from home, a Big Orange Drink, and a big bag of popcorn, which I shared with Spud in one of his favorite bowls. Had a blanket in case the temperature dropped which it was known to do that time of year. Space in my Rumble Seat for a girl if one should happen along looking for a place to sit to watch the movie with me and Spud. She would have to sit real close to me to get into the seat.

The movie was "Ride the High Country" with Randolph Scott, and Joel McCrea, a western of course. Must have been 1963 when this movie came out and made its way down to little old Yuma. One Dollar a carload made the movies a family affair, and on any Saturday Night, the place was usually packed.

The Movie just got started when a couple of my rowdy friends pulled in right next to us and got out with their lawn chairs to join us. They had beer of course but were none too eager to share it with me. I didn't care to drink somewhat room-temperature beer, so it didn't matter to me. Spud didn't care he was fast asleep by my side. Wasn't long before I had to pee and of course, old Spud went with me. At the snake bar, I met a girl I knew from school and we talked a bit. Very much out of my element talking to a girl I hardly knew. She was there alone and said she'd love to join me and Spud back at my car. Turns out she had come to the Drive-In and didn't bring a jacket with her so she was shivering a bit as the temperature had indeed dropped some since the evening began. Back at the car Old Spud went to his new place in the front seat of the car and he curled up to go back to sleep. My friends had left and their car was gone as well. Me and Beth squeezed into the seat in the back of my car and pulled the blanket over us and found the warmth to be very comforting to both of us as we somewhat watched the movie together. I knew her name was Beth and we had several classes together at school but really had only ever said Hello and Goodby in passing. Beth was very pretty and had developed into a lovely young woman in all the right places that a boy would notice. I remember her living about 6 or 7 blocks from the Drive-In, in a neighborhood where I used to deliver Newspapers. Seemed like a long walk home in the cool of the evening that night so I told her I would drive her home after the show. She said that would be very nice. Her mother had dropped her off at the Drive-In and she was definitely not looking forward to walking home in the cold. We mostly talked about school, classes, teachers, and other people we knew, which was a very short list for me. Don't remember much about the movie cause I was much more interested in this girl than any movie ever made.

I was 16 going on 17 years old and thinking about girls all the time. I truly did want to kiss Beth and I was hoping she wanted me to kiss her too. I was just working up to the event when the movie ended and everyone was leaving. I was very disappointed at my lack of courage and she seemed let down as well. But I almost made up for it by taking her down to the Tip Top Car Hop Drive-In on 4th Avenue for a Cherry Coke and a Grilled Cheese Sandwich. Looked like everyone was there and she got to be seen with me and that in my opinion was great. Old Spud was in the back seat such as it was and gave us little attention. Everyone we saw spoke to her and no one even acknowledged me. I was not a school person and never had been. Not into sports or any school activities cause I was gone all the time doing my Rodeo thing, which no one knew about. Before you knew it it was time for me to take Beth home and she was amazed that I drove right up to her front door without asking where she lived. I told her I was once her paperboy and remember seeing her when I would come to her house to collect for the paper. She said she didn't remember me at all. I said that is definitely the norm, as I am a nobody both in and out of school. She thanked me for sharing time with her and keeping her warm. Appreciated the Grilled Cheese and Coke, and that the next time it would be her turn to buy. Then she kissed me. Oh Lord, she kissed me. I thought I would melt. Next thing I knew she was out of the car and standing at her front door. The door opened and she was gone.

Many thoughts raced through my mind as I sat there. Was it me, was it the cool of the evening, was it my blanket, or the fact that I offered a warm place to sit to watch the movie? Was the Tip Top the reason for the kiss?

I figured it all out in my head and came up with her giving me a kiss was on her mind as strongly as it was on mine. Just a spur-of-the-moment thing and really meant nothing in the big scheme of things, unless I followed up on it.

On Monday I looked for her at school and wanted desperately to move forward with what I thought was a relationship. Giving me the kiss that she did was a clear indication that she wanted me to get to know her better. She was not there at school that day. After school, I drove to her house but got no response at the door. I drove back to the school and went to the office to find out what I could. That's when I got the news. Beth was killed in a traffic accident on Sunday, driving home with her family from El Cento, California. The word had not yet spread throughout the school. My high expectation of our getting together was crushed as was my thinking about the events of the last few days. Although as tragic as it was about the death of Beth, my concern was about me and my loss. Seems we always put ourselves before others when we think about the life we are living. What should have been, what could have been, have always followed me from those events on those days so long ago.

Rumors spread through out the school that Beth and I were involved and had a very secretive love affair going on. This came from our being seen together that Saturday Night down at the Tip Top. I didn't know who to tell it was not true, nor did I think they would believe me. What people think is way beyond our control. I can't say I was viewed differently from that time on by the other kids in school. Certainly, I had changed but I don't think they saw that.

A Saturday Night at the Drive-In Movie with my dog Spud. A chance encounter with a beautiful girl, and time to spend with her although brief.

A snapshot of life and the closing of a door for me. I would go through many types of loss in the years I have been alive. Not all of the pain involved the death of someone, but many did. Heartbreak is hard to take, but in time it does lessen in pain. Never forgotten but easier to take.

Momma's Cup

It had been some weeks ago that she told me the story of the gift she received from Dad. As she told me about it I began to remember little bits and pieces that were buried in my youth. She was thinking about a silver cup that she used to own. As she talked about it she cupped her old and worn hands as if holding that cup again. Maybe it was not really silver maybe it was just some sort of metal, no matter about that, she said. It was hers and she treasured that cup as if it were the very chalice used by Jesus to drink at the last supper. Over the years she had misplaced it or lost it along the way and it bothered her enough that she now talked about it. Maybe as we grow in years those things we cherished most become important again, at least to our way of thinking they do. As far as I could tell from her description of the cup it was very plain and was just a cup with no finger hold or base. She said the color inside was different from the outside color and that everything tasted so much better with that cup. She said for a fact that cool water tastes wonderful from a simple unpainted or un-enameled metal cup. The feel of the metal in your hand, the touch of the metal to your lips, and the sensation that this is really how water should taste is rare and lives in one's memory. Hot drinks burn you and cold drinks sweat in metal cups, but cool water in a metal cup is a thing reserved for wonderment. She remembers drinking water drawn from a well. Oh how fresh and clean the taste of the water from deep below, and how refreshing to just sip from that cup. She said if she could find it she would like to drink from it again.

That's when I told her what I had found in that old leather foot locker of Dad's that I came by somewhere down the way. It was wrapped in an old shirt stuffed back in the corner under some other clothes and not noticed for some years. I didn't know it was hers till she mentioned it, but I brought it to her so she could have it again and keep it with her always. Her eyes lit up like a child at Christmas at the sight of the cup. I had polished it to its highest gloss, and it truly was silver. As she took the cup in her trembling hands she was smiling as big as I had ever seen. This was her cup and it was now home for her to hold.

I poured her some cool water into the cup from a bottle of store-bought water thinking it would taste better than old tap water, and she sipped it. She just smiled and held her cup with both hands, as tears started to fill her eyes I knew she was happy. She sat in silence for the longest time. I knew she was gone away from here to a place she once knew and she was there again in the shade, sipping cool water from her cup. I didn't want to disturb her or take her away from those fond memories that she holds so dear, but I wondered if Dad was with her in her remembered journey. I didn't ask, I just assumed he was.

As she sat and looked out the window, I knew she was there with him somewhere and they were just so happy and content to be with each other again. She then looked at me and said "Your father gave me this cup the day he asked me to marry him. Didn't have no ring for my finger, but he had this here cup. Said we may not have all we ever want, but a cool drink of water will go a long way to make a body feel good. I took his cup and I took his hand in marriage. Proud to have both. He got a divorced woman and two boys in the bargain" Momma told me she never had a wedding ring till she had been married for about 10 years to that old boy. Said "Money for that sort of thing just weren't in our budget. Even when he did buy me a ring it weren't very much money, and it didn't fit real good neither." She still wears it to this day and wouldn't take it off for her life. She says "he weren't no prize you know. Had to keep him in line many a time over the years. Headstrong and stubborn but he was a good man, bent on working hard to make a living, and we did just fine. Your daddy never was one to drink whiskey and I admired him for that. He could fix anything and he kept himself clean. I worked at keeping him a good house and made him a good wife. Wished he didn't hate those church-going people as much as he did. Never thought me nor this here cup would outlive that old boy, but we did.... he sure loved that game of Golf" she said "told me when I get to heaven to look him up on the big Golf course in the sky, he'd be playing with some real pro's up there " Then she drifted off somewhere and was looking out the window for the longest time. I didn't say anything or interrupt her--after all, it wasn't my journey.

Momma has her cup and she can drink from it anytime she wants to. Makes me think about my own drinking cup and where it is. Do you have one somewhere? If you think about it, we all have a cup like that somewhere and we can use it anytime we want to, to go back to those days that were the best of all of them. Not everyone has a silver cup like momma, but we all have dreams and memories.

Dreams and memories are the best silver cups.

My Father's Gift

9 Years Old

On winter mornings in Yuma, the wind comes howling and cuts right through clothing to chill a person right down to the bone. Winter brings great memories for me of my childhood and Christmas time in that house.

I can remember those times as if they were here right now. Cold mornings that could only be handled by standing near Momma's cook stove in the kitchen of that small house. Momma would be cooking up something to feed everyone and my father would be drinking coffee, smoking his pipe, and reading the morning paper.

The house was a small brick house on the mesa just outside of that desert town. A tract of homes were built after World War II so that veterans like my father could afford to buy a house. Being a fireman for the city didn't pay a great deal back then but the work was steady. We didn't have a lot of things that other folks had, but what we did have was a sense of worth brought about by doing things together. My father was a great fixer and we didn't need an electrician, plumber, carpenter, or anything else, because he could and would fix it if it broke or didn't work right. If something needed painting we did it together. If one of us three boys broke a pane of glass we would get a whipping for sure, but then we would get some education on how to fix the window, giving worth to the repair.

My father believed that things needed to have value or worth to spend time or money on them, so there were not a lot of frills in our home. One of the things that he did not see of value was spending money on a cut and dying tree from far away to put into our home for Christmas. Oh, he allowed it some of the time, but grudgingly and not with any degree of Christmas Spirit. Christmas trees did not grow on the desert; and being the avid outdoorsman that he was, he needed a sense of place and time.

It must have been about 1956 when my father began a tradition that lived in our home for many years. We don't know how he got the idea or from where, but one Christmas he did something different. He went out on the desert and selected a shapely Tumble Weed. He brought the thing home and worked on it for several days. The Tumble Weed was approximately 4 feet wide and about 5 feet tall. After a bit of trimming he built a stand for it using an empty gallon can of paint filled with rock and sand, so it would stand up straight and true.

Next came the paint. Using spray paint and glitter to stick to the wet paint, he made a Christmas Tree in the Desert. Once inside the home, we all joined in gathering ornaments to hang on our Tumbleweed Tree. We used needle and thread to put popcorn and cranberries together to wrap around the tree, and Dad even strung some lights on the tree to give it life. Mom had Christmas Cards hung on a length of fishing line behind the tree and there was always a Nativity Scene set up for all to see.

During the Christmas Season friends and neighbors would come by to see the Christmas Tree of the Desert and all of them marveled at how perfect and beautiful it was.

Christmas Eve our family gathered around the tree and sang carols to welcome the birthday of the Baby Jesus. My father always kept the music going with his guitar. We had hot chocolate and Christmas Pie which mom would take right out of the oven and serve hot. Sometimes she would really give us a treat and make homemade donuts sprinkled with sugar, or even oatmeal cookies.

I know the meaning of love, family, togetherness, and Christmas. I know that a simple desert weed can provide the greatest joy in the world to a boy growing up in a home where true values are made a part of life.

I remember momma's cooking, the cold concrete floors of that brick house, the warmth of the cooking stove, and the smell of dad's pipe. These things and more made that house a home. I have seen many Christmas Trees in my life that would be greatly valued for their beauty. None of them will ever compare to the Tumbleweed Tree of the Desert that my fathers gave us on that Christmas in Yuma so many years ago.

Christmas in a Desert Town

Always seems to start long ago and far away for me when I write about Christmas as a boy in my hometown. Christmas on the desert where I lived was a special time of year. It would get cold and the wind would blow to move the sand along as it always does. The nights were long and the days were short but the Sun would shine no matter the time of day. Seasons for me were all about the length of the day and how far away the Sun felt on my skin at Christmas. There were really only two seasons in my hometown, Hotter than the Hubs of Hell, and downright nice. Although the temperature was great for Sun Bathing at Christmas it was better than 120 degrees in the shade for the people that lived there year-round.

Christmas meant the family came home to be together for that special day each year. The Christmas that always comes to me in my dreams is the one in 1964 when Jimmy, my oldest brother came with his wife and little girl. Billy, the next oldest boy came with his wife and little boy. I had my girlfriend at the time with me and it would be a wonderful day cause it was my 18th birthday on December 25. Dad was a fireman for the city and normally worked 24 hours on and 24 hours off, but on this day the guys took turns at work so everyone could have time at home for the Christmas meal. Dad would have time with us to eat and be with the kids but had to go back to work after a while. Mom was a nurse at the hospital and had her duties there to attend to and was always on call for emergencies during that time of year.

So the time we did have together was special for all of us.

I had joined the US Navy and was set to leave for boot camp on the 24th of January, 1965. I finished High School in 1964 and realized I had no future in that little town on the desert so the Navy was my way to grow up and learn about the great big world I lived in.

Soon the day would end as always with the brothers gathering up their stuff and heading for home. Everyone had to work the next day and I was no exception. Working again at the Blakley's Gas Station as I had done several times over the years. Pumping gas and selling oil, and tires, was my professional life so far in my 18 years in Yuma, with no prospects of doing better.

Mom would cry as her boys left for their homes. Dad was gone back to work by then. I was back home after taking my girlfriend back to her place as well. Mom and I would set and talk about the future and how it would eventually play out. I would go into the Navy and the folks would be the empty nesters that they knew they would be one day. My brothers both lived in California, so seeing them would be hit-and-miss at best, if at all. Dad wanted to travel once he retired from the fire department and Mom said she would retire from nursing at the same time as Dad no matter what.

I had Christmas Eve off from my work but was set to go to my shift at 11:00 pm on Christmas Night. It was about 8:00 pm when Mom got the call of a major emergency at the hospital involving a serious car wreck out on the highway. She was gone in just a minute or two and I was there alone in that house on my birthday with nothing but thoughts of family and my life as lived thus far in that Desert Town. I didn't know what my life would be like in 50 years if I made it that far into the future. I wondered then as I wonder now, what is it all about. How will I remember these times? How will I look back on these years? Will growing older make me see the life as I have lived it, any clearer? I made myself a cup of coffee and sat at the dining room table thinking about things that would come and things that had passed. Not much distinction between the two so far in 18 years.

As I sat there I thought about Billy and our times in rodeo over the years. I thought about Jimmy the oldest of us boys and how I never really got to know him, since he was gone from home by the time I even knew who I was. Dad and Mom and the time they put into making me the boy I was, who wanted to be a man and prove I had grown up. I thought about my girlfriend and how in a few days I would more than likely never see her again. Let me add, that was one of the clearer thoughts that I had at the time and was so very true.

I walked out in the yard of that house on Cactus Drive and looked up at the stars and wondered if the same stars would follow me in the years to come. I knew they would but I would not know it at the time as I would become busy with my life. That too was a true thought as it turns out but really only has occurred to me here lately at a much older age. It was by then time to go to work at the gas station and really to move on to the path I had chosen to follow in the near future.

Here is the place where I discuss Jimmy, my oldest half-brother. He didn't like me deciding to join the US Navy and made it real clear that it was a mistake and a stupid thing to do. We almost had a fistfight over the issue but he left with his wife and daughter and that was that. I must say the bond between Jimmy and me was not strong and in the 36 years that followed that Christmas in 1964 I never saw him again nor did I ever speak to him. Jimmy passed away in 2000 and I didn't know about that until some days later. To say we were strangers would be an understatement, and certainly not brothers, even with the common bond of the same mother. I never knew the man and so I can't begin to tell in the smallest way how I miss him or ever missed him in my life.

Billy was my brother and my closest friend throughout my adolescent years. Billy encouraged me to try my hand at rodeo and kept me going even when things didn't go well, or I got hurt, which happened from time to time. I'd like to think I developed an ability to endure pain along the way as I grew into doing what I felt I had a calling to do. Some people say there are those who have a natural ability to ride a Bronc and ride them well. I had to learn how to ride, how to find the rhythm, how to deal with the hurt involved with failure, and even the pain of success. It isn't a lack of fear that drives a person to strive for perfection in the art of Bronc Riding, it is knowing full well that it can happen at any moment but still going for the 8-second count. To me, it was the full measure of reaching for a high goal and achieving it with a lot of failures along the way. Billy was my mentor and kept me going when it looked like all was lost. We were close and stayed in touch always with and through Mom till he passed away in 2011.

Dad and Mom enjoyed retirement together for some 25 years before Dad passed away in 2001. Mom was strong and carried on with her life as a widow for another 13 years before passing away in 2014. I was very happy to have my current wife Georgia involved in the care of Mom for 7 years before Mom went to her heavenly reward. Christmas was always my birthday, and I was proud all my life to share it with Jesus in a Desert Place.

Out In The Gila Valley

5 Years Old

Out in the Gila Valley from Yuma, was the Ferguson spread. My Aunt Beatrice was my father's older sister by 17 years. She had come to Yuma in 1922 as the Laguna District school teacher. " Aunt Bea " as she was always known to me married Frank Merrifield Ferguson Sr., of that area a prominent Rancher and Farmer. Frank Ferguson was always known to me as Uncle Fergie or just Fergie. Robert Burley Sparks was born in 1918, my father, came to Yuma, to be with his older sister Bea, and to work for Frank Ferguson on his farm in about 1935. As I found out later my father's older brother Gordon Wesley Sparks, about two years younger than Aunt Bea, was living in Yuma, renting a house on 5th Avenue and working as an auto mechanic at a place called The Public Garage. In 1938 my father joined the U.S. Army and stayed till the end of WWII getting out and coming to Yuma again in 1945, with my mother Annie Mae Watson Thompson Sparks, and her two sons Jimmy and Billy. Dad needed work to support his family and again went to work for Frank Ferguson Sr. as a farm and ranch hand.

Then Dad got an offer of work in town paying him a much better wage than Fergie was paying him, so he took the job and became an Auto Mechanic at Bristow Brothers Dodge Chrysler Desoto dealership, 3rd Street and 5th Avenue

I came along in December of 1946 and always lived in the city of Yuma, as far as I know. We would visit the Ferguson's out in the Gila Valley often, as my father was always partial to his older sister and she of him since he was the baby in the Sparks family. Spending time out on the farm and ranch gave me a lot of time to see and learn about life out in this place.

My earliest recollections of farm life was from the perspective of a 5-year-old boy. Aunt Bea was a big woman and always cooking something in her kitchen, which smelled wonderful. They had a well from which they got their water and it tasted so good I just couldn't drink enough of it. Great big Fig Trees were all across the back side of their property mixed in with Grapefruit and Orange Trees. The fallen leaves from these trees were thick on the ground in that area between cuttings with a tractor which Uncle Fergie did from time to time. The trees were perfect for climbing and as a boy, it was my job to climb every one of them. Falling out of the trees was part and parcel of that job for me but I always landed on a thick mat of fallen leaves which would break my fall. I learned how to eat Figs while out and among them. My brother Billy said the Green Figs would give me the runs and I soon found out even the Brown Figs would give me the runs. Knowing what was going to happen to me as a result of eating the Figs, I ate them anyway.

Spending time out on the farm I got to know Uncle Fergie pretty good and learned his ways. One thing Uncle Fergie was known for was his language which was very colorful, to say the least. He always had a cuss word or two in every sentence he spoke. I liked it cause it was different to me and sounded downright good. My mother on the other hand hated the words Uncle Fergie would use in his speech and would tell me constantly not to pay attention to Uncle Fergie's language and to speak right. Fergie was a rough-and-tumble kind of guy used to hard work on a farm and was not kind in his choice of words when he talked about it. I took in every word Uncle Fergie would say and he liked me cause I was attentive and listened.

One day I spent the afternoon with Uncle Fergie down at the corrals tending to some cattle he had along with several horses. I would guess I was 6 or 7 years old at that time. I got schooled on feeding and cleaning up after the animals and other odd jobs as they came along. Once we killed a nest of Cow Killers, as Fergie called them.

Said they were bad to have around and he showed me how to get rid of them using Kerosene and a lighted rag on the end of a long pole.

Later on in life, I learned about these critters and found out they were Wasps and bad for farm animals of all types. Seems the females of this type of Wasp don't have wings and crawl on the ground making them easy to stomp on. The kind Uncle Fergie had were Yellow and Back stripped and very hairy. I would stomp on them for him and he told me I was doing God's work for him. I asked how it was God's work and Fergie would tell me "Those sons a bitches is straight out of Hell and God wants us to kill em." My mother asked me later that night what me and Fergie had done that day and I told her about burning the critters down at the corrals. She asked what Uncle Fergie was teaching me about the upkeep of the area around the animals as if I was supposed to learn about animal husbandry in some fashion or another. I told her what Uncle Fergie had taught me about Cow Killers as being " those sons a bitches is straight out a Hell and God wants us to kill 'em." My mother was not happy at all and said I was not to talk like Uncle Fergie. Several times she got onto Fergie for his language and he would say he'd watch it around the kids, but he never did. We loved him for it.

Billy loved catching crawdads down in the spillway off the levee. Used to catch a big bucket of them critters and I was very much aware of his prowess as a crawdad catcher. Used to look at his catch and say, what are you going to do with them now that you have them in your bucket? Billy would say we're going to cook em up and eat them. Growing up I pretty much figured my brother Billy would not lead me into trouble or give me bad advice, but eating those bugs was not on the list of things I would adhere to. I never did and to this day I will not. Crawdads and Frog Gigging were two things I did not do with my brother Billy while out at the farm. Uncle Fergie said crawdads were " God Dam fine food for a starving boy " and said I was not eating enough at home. I told my dad that crawdads were " God Dam fine food " according to Uncle Fergie, and he told me they weren't and to stop cussing.

Uncle Fergie always called me by his pet name for me "Poop Stain". I guess he figured I was young enough to take a name like that without getting upset about it, he was right. I once made the mistake of calling him Mr. Ferguson. He told me never to do that again or he'd hit me on my head so hard he'd likely break his hand. Fergie was a smoker and a drinker which made my mother very uneasy to be around him. But my father was very attached to Aunt Bea and Uncle Fergie for many reasons, like giving him a job when he needed one and a place to live. Learned about working on tractors and trucks while working for Fergie. Then honed those skills in the US Army for eight years. By the time War broke out my father was already a

Sergeant, stationed in Paris, Texas. You know the rest of the story as it played out for the family in Yuma.

Breakfast

I can't say how old I was when I started following him around. Maybe because he was old and slow and I never feared being left behind. He would walk around finding things that needed mending and then go to his workbench in the old carport. Always smoking his pipe even if a coat of varnish was needed on one thing or another. I watched and I learned as best I could by watching what he did. Slow and deliberate were his moves as if to give me a chance to see what he was doing. Every now and then he would stop and look at me to see if I was paying attention or if I was asleep. I never asked him any questions cause I didn't know what to ask. He never gave me a lecture and just did what he did without worrying about me.

Day after day the routine was always the same. Shaved on Tuesday and Saturday unless it was Monday or Friday. Whenever the mood stuck him he would up and shave. Used a straight razor and strop with an old cup and brush. Didn't worry about being complete, just got most of the hair off his face. Flannel shirt, bib overalls, and great big oversized boots with laces that were never tied. An old slouch hat with a bird feather or two shoved into the outside hat band. With pipe in hand, we were ready for another adventure around the old place. Rain or shine, heat or cold, we were out and about checking on one thing or another.

Black Coffee in an old cup that was dirty and stained. He said that cup had been to breakfast. He used that term " been to breakfast " with anything that was used and dull, in particular knives. If the blade of a knife was dull he referred to it as having been to breakfast. Simple for me to understand at my age and conveyed the meaning that it needed to be fixed. Taking the time to sharpen a blade was always easy for him. Never was in a hurry to do anything but always got it done.

I was in diapers when we first started hanging around together down at his home on 9th Avenue in Yuma. After a while, I stopped needing diapers and followed him around wearing nothing but a smile. He would finally say I needed me some clothes on so I could sit on wood without splinters being a part of my day. Had me a pair of shorts and I wore them out wearing them day after day.

Watering the flowers was a daily activity in the front yard. We would water and he would point out weeds that I would pull. We had a very nice garden also and we would pull or cut vegetables as needed for our lunch.

After lunch, we would sit on the front screened-in porch and he would tune in the radio to music and sit for hours carving animals out of wood. I would take a nap as always and dream about the music in the background as I heard it. I realize that 40's swing music is ingrained in me and I love it because of my hearing it in my sleep for the longest time as a child. To me, it is the music of a golden age. A war was being fought and men were dying. Spirits were high and emotions were strong. A music that makes me feel secure and safe whenever I hear it. The music of my youth.

Grandpa always had a way of speaking to me that I understood even at a time in my life when adults were a mystery. He would say things to me like watch your step as you go through life. Sometimes holes will appear in your shoes and you need to take the time to fix it. If not you will be doing wrong and hurt will come to you. Hurt will find you when you least expect it. Got to be careful to not ask for hurt at any time. Sometimes he would tell me about people. Going to buy something from a man count his fingers. Butchers don't always have all of their fingers. Don't mean they can't cut meat. Bankers think about nothing but money and your money is the most important money of all. Always look for the other eye. Most people are one-eyed jacks to us. We only see what they show us to see. Look for the other eye to know the real person that they are. Man says he has all the answers, you need to walk away from him. Watch, listen, and read, to find the real truth. The past is not gone, we carry it with us as we go. Anytime you need to refer to the past it's right here. Growing old does not mean gaining wisdom. Gramps said he knew a lot of people that were getting older and were still stupid and always would be. Ignorant means they don't know better. Stupid means they know better but still do wrong.

Earliest memories for me were of being with that old man. I don't remember ever saying anything to him and that seemed to be fine with him. In later years we would sit and talk about stuff he knew about. Life was a simple matter for him and he didn't worry about anything. Gramps always said if you worry about something or someone you're actually saying God can't handle the situation and it's praying on your mind. Stop the worry and realize God is capable more so than any person on earth. God moves at his own pace and knows best the right time to get things done. I asked Gramps if Grandma knew what he did about worry and God. He said she never did understand about that and was a real worry wart. Said she gave him 9 kids and didn't complain about it much, so he figured he'd overlook her shortcomings. I asked if he loved her and he said he did care a great deal for her off and on over the years, but love is a hard thing to pin down. Gramps said he loved a pair of mules once and they were a right fine brace. But loving a woman wasn't easy on a man, less he worked at it awful hard. Most times it just wasn't worth the trouble. I knew the words he spoke to me, but his view did not turn out to be my view. That old saying tell me something and I will forget just didn't apply to what Grandpa said to me. I loved him without knowing I did.

Overcoming Fear

I was about 5 years old when I first started watching my grandfather do the things he did. By that time of his life, he had already raised 9 kids to adults and had many grandchildren. I was the youngest grandchild he had from his youngest son, and for one reason or another as I'm sure is common with young boys, I idolized that old man. He was a big burly man somewhat stooped over in the shoulders but still spry and capable of doing things around a farm. He had enormous hands as I recall. Big hands that were strong, hard, and heavily callused from years of hard work. He was old and everything he had was old too. He still shaved with a straight razor every time he shaved depending on his nerve as he would say. Some mornings he was a bit shaky till he had a cup or two of coffee. Coffee was meant to be drank black as night out of an old blue tin cup. I watched him many a morning as he got his coffee he would walk outside and just stand and stare off into space. I asked him once what he was thinking about and he said "Old horses, sweet women, fine whiskey, n' friends".

He always wore old patched and sewn coveralls with a red bandanna sticking out of a rear pocket. These he wore over a long-sleeved plaid shirt of some faded color which had been sewn up many times over. Lace-up boots without any socks, said it's not easy to step into socks as it is a good old pair of shoes. An old slouch hat, and as he called it a "crook stem pipe" with a metal cover on the bowl, most times lit and always in his mouth, would generally round out his attire.

He always carried a pocket knife. The large double-bladed type that had been sharpened over many years and was in fact as sharp as a razor. "Knife that's been to breakfast ain't worth spit in a man's pocket" he would say. I once took that knife out by myself and was playing with it for a while till I cut the heck out of myself and put it back where he had laid it. He looked at my cut and said "I've another un here I'll give you and it's already stoned to cut. Trick is to see if you can keep it working without losing a finger". I still have that knife and I might add I have all my fingers. A gold pocket watch on a gold chain was usually hanging from his breast pocket. You know the kind with a cover on it that when opened showed the picture of a woman. I always thought it was Grandma but I never asked.

A hard plug of tobacco was always there somewhere too, as he loved a good chew now and again. "Store-bought teeth don't stop a man from simple stuff such as this" he would say and showed me the plug he carried. Heavy and dark was the tobacco he would chew and once worked up to it he was a dead-on shot when he would spit. The top of my head from several yards off was no problem for him to hit, and it seemed like a favorite target. My mother would get very hateful at Grandpa when she had to wash dried tobacco juice out of my hair. I do believe it is the main reason I can't grow hair on the top of my head today.

One morning I found Grandpa standing in front of the old barn with the open door. He was studying something and I couldn't tell right off what it was. I walked up to him and asked what he was doing. "Watch here boy and get yer self some learning" he said. He was staring up into the rafters of the old barn and I could clearly see the object of his concern. There attached to one of the support beams at the top of the barn was the largest Hornets Nest I had ever seen. It might have seemed larger because of my size, and in my mind, I'm sure it grew larger over the years. It was big, none the less, and those critters as he called them flying around it were the problem. These insects were big and dark in color and no doubt at all they were Hornets. They made considerable noise when flying in a group and they were out and about on that day.

Now bear in mind these insects were very strong and upon getting a hold on you they were not easily dislodged. With the equipment God gave them which "hung out of their rear like a pitchfork handle", as he would say, they could hurt you bad and often. We are talking about the ability to stick that razor-sharp stinger right through leather and not even slow down to do it.

I noticed an old ladder leaning up to that beam and I saw that Grandpa had a small handsaw in his right hand. This must have been a special occasion cause the crook stem pipe was gone from his mouth and he was chewing his plug tobacco. I then saw a 55-gallon drum some yards off with a fire burning in it. The drum had holes poked in the sides down low so the air could get in and he had a roaring fire going with flames licking up out of the top. "You're my sidekick in this war so stay close," he said, "and do as I say".

About that time those hornets must have called a meeting cause they all went inside that nest. All that is except one and he was perched on the outside of the nest sort of like a sentry. That's when Grandpa took off up that ladder. Slow and deliberate were his steps and I could see he kept his eye on the nest as he was climbing.

Soon he was within range and he took a quick step up and spit at the same time. Accurate as always and he took that sentry right off of that nest and down he came to the floor of the barn. At the same time, Grandpa shoved his left thumb right up into the opening to the nest. He then turned to me and said

"Boy, you get over there, find that critter and stomp the life out of him".

I got over close to that creature on the barn floor and I could tell he was mad cause he was making a lot of noise and had that tobacco juice all over him. I wanted nothing to do with this deal and I especially didn't want to get close to that thing on the floor of the barn.

"You better do what I said right quick, soon as he gets his wings a working he's going to find you".

I stomped that bug till it quit moving cause I believed in Grandpa.

"Now that's right smart, and here's another thing you might note. Don't take your thumb out of this here hole".

Hey, I wouldn't have put my thumb in that hole to start with. With those words said, Grandpa began sawing at the top of the nest and when it broke loose he dropped the hand saw and held tight to the nest. I dodged that saw and heard him say

"You'd be smart not to drop this here, cause boy I got hell and damnation wadded up in a ball right here".

Then he eased his way down that old ladder. Once on the ground, he walked up to me with that nest held tightly in his hands and I could hear those Hornets rumbling inside that big hunk of twigs and leaves. I don't know what Hornets sound like when they are happy, but I do know what they sound like when they are upset. Something like a 35-horse outboard motor just a rumbling at an idle.

Grandpa then walked over to that fire and dropped the nest into it and took a couple of steps back as the fire roared and consumed his offering.

I walked up to Grandpa and took hold of his hand and looked at his old and gnarled thumb.

"Grandpa didn't those bugs sting your thumb".

"No, as he held up his thumb for me, 'cause they don't know what that is".

"Were they touching your thumb"?

"Sure they were pushing and pulling to get me to move it".

"How about wearing a glove? "

"No, they'd know right off that was a glove and your thumb would be stitched up like a Sewing Machine had got ya and hurt real bad".

I knew somehow he had been in the position of dealing with these bugs before and had been on the losing end of the process.

As Grandpa said many times to me "The shovel you were given at birth is a big one, the best way to deal with it is small loads till you can handle a full load. Some folks never get to the full load. You will know them by that."

As we stood there watching the fire burn, he didn't say anything to me. I had been taught how to deal with what life gives us and I was happy.

Later on that day I saw my father and told him what I had helped Grandpa do. My father grabbed me up and shook me so hard I thought my head was going to come off as he said "You stay away from that old man, he's going to get you hurt".

Many years later I recounted this tale to my father and asked him if he didn't do some of these things with Grandpa. He said he watched that old man do things that a normal man would never do. Grandpa did not know fear as we know it mainly because of need. Those Hornets needed to be removed and fear had no place in his actions.

I told that story to a fellow once who was an insect man of some renown and he said he could explain why the Hornets didn't sting Grandpa. You see these insects smear a substance at the opening of their nest and going in and out cover themselves with their nesting scent. He used a real fancy word like Pheromone or something like that. So he believes that when Grandpa shoved his thumb up in the nest he covered his thumb with the scent from the opening and the Hornets did not recognize the thumb as an enemy. I wonder if Grandpa knew all this stuff.

I said Learning hasn't occurred until behavior changes. I'm still learning cause any time I am around Hornets or "critters" that make noise when they fly my behavior has not changed. I don't think about ladders, or hand saws, or 55-gallon drums on fire. I do what most people do and start swatting at them and running for cover. Fear takes over right away and the cool thinking of doing these rascals in, is not the first thought on my mind.

I do think about what causes men to fear. The reason we fear is a need or the lack of it. If we have a strong enough need we can overcome fear. Grandpa had figured that out and in his way he had showed me how to be smarter than those critters. He had showed me how to overcome fear.

Reason Enough

I have come to find that bad days don't always start out bad. Some even start out good for a while and get better before they go bad. This was one of those good days that went along real good getting better then went down in a hurry. It was a hot day and the sun was directly overhead casting shadows straight down. The temperature was on high bake and the cooking element felt about 12 inches from my head even with my pithy pith helmet on, which Granddad had given me. Temperature that day would have been around the 115 mark or a bit higher in the shade, which we were not in. The desert was very still without anything moving at all except me and old Spud. The sand being hot didn't matter to Spud. He knew a swim was coming at the end of our adventure, down in the shade of a large stand of cottonwood trees off the mesa at the crosscut canal. The very canal my dad had taught me to swim in when I was just a pup myself. That was before I had the itch to hunt and didn't care about being alone or with that old shaggy dog. Seems we always went swimming even if we didn't find anything to shoot at. Didn't much care for the company of others at the public pool down off 5th Avenue. Besides this swimming was free and I could go in with Spud, who they said couldn't go in the public pool. He smelled a lot better than most of those kids at that pool, and he had better manners. One thing about that pool was you had to shower before they would let you in, and everything smelled like chlorine. I didn't mind paying the 25 cents to go in but I minded being in a crowd. Down at the canal old Spud and me were the only ones around. The signs saying not to swim in the canal were ignored by a few brave souls like me and Spud. I know what you're thinking, having seen bullet holes in signs like that, but we didn't do that sort of thing.

I wasn't thinking of nothing when it happened, it just happened. The hurt began to set in right away and it was getting to be intense. I could feel the swelling cause my boot was getting real tight. Just above the ankle on my left leg, two puncture wounds. Went right through my good pair of boots. Didn't see him and I rarely missed seeing them. Spud missed him too and that was real rare. Came right out of a greasewood bush and went right for me. Spud went crazy jumping and barking, soon as the snake bit me. Got me on the first of two strikes and I'm glad he missed the second time. First order of business was to kill the snake, which I did. Second order was to get my boot off, but I waited till I got to the Third order of business before doing that.

Third order was getting to that cool shady place, which was at the canal down off the Mesa. Only had to walk about a quarter of a mile or so. Wasn't hard to walk knowing where and what I was about. Didn't worry till I saw what was coming. I had tied off my leg just above the knee with my belt just to slow down the movement of snake juice toward my heart, and it was beginning to ache really bad. My boot didn't want to come off right away, and I had to cut the laces to get my foot free. Thought for a moment there I'd have to cut the boot and didn't want to do that. Not for no low-down sneaking snake. Good boots are important you know. I eased my knife down to open the bite marks a bit with it, but it hurt too much to be cutting on. Had a good amount of blood in my boot so I figured it was running out fluid blood and venom pretty good. Got my foot down in the cool running water and it sure felt good. Didn't have to hardy ease down the bank at all to get to the water. The canal was running a good head of water that day and almost to the brim. Canal was a good fifty feet wide at that spot and would run fifteen to twenty feet deep in spots. The big old cottonwood trees covered most of the area around there and shade was thick and nice. The place I was sitting on was all grass and felt good to sit and lay back for a bit. Spud liked me to get in the water first every time but if I took too long he'd hit it. His favorite trick was to get out in the current and just paddle fast enough to keep in one place for a while. As I remember back to that time I don't remember old Spud being around me at all as I lay there. I don't know why old Spud left me but he sure was gone. That's when I formulated the Fourth Order of business, which was fast becoming the First Order, not dying. I remember laying there thinking about all the girls that would one day ask about the marks on my ankle and wonder what it's like to get snake bit. I was thirsty but didn't want any water. I wanted to stand and walk but I couldn't. I wanted to yell that I needed help but I couldn't. All I could do was wait for whatever was coming.

My ankle was hurting sure enough, and not numb like I had heard so many times before about snake bites. Been bit twice before and each time it was a bit different for me to deal with. I was about a 5-mile walk from home and had been told many times to remain calm, sit down and wait for help to come. I knew that if I didn't pass out or die in the next hour that I would be alright. At least that was in my mind as I sat there sweating more than normal. There on the bank of the canal with my leg in the water made me think about the times Spud and I have been out on the desert with no real excitement at all. The real concern in my mind is that the snake could have bit Spud, and that would have been bad. He would get all sick and lay around for a week or so and then get better, instead of swimming around in the canal and having fun. Dogs just get real sick, they rarely die from snake bites. I found out early on that hogs will kill a snake and eat it. They too are immune to snake bites, but not us humans that don't pay enough attention to what we're doing.

As I sat there I kept thinking that my life is supposed to pass before me if it's my time to die. Hadn't lived that long to have much pass by and if it did I missed it cause it would have been a short parade with only one float. I kept thinking about that one float and what it might be. That's when I imagined old Spud up on the float barking at everybody as it passed by. He was wet and muddy from being in the canal. Then I noticed I was too. Maybe that's why we have events happen in our lives, so we can have them reappear as we need them when we die. Some aren't worth remembering and those are the ones that seem to crowd us at times like that. This was one of those events I'd just as soon forget and never remember. Thought about Mom, and how mad she would be with me, and the fact that I got in trouble. Dad won't let me use the rifle anymore and I'd sure like a drink of water or something like that. Thought about Jesus, and how it was one of his critters that bit me. Since he made the snake I guessed it was his way of saying " Here's an event for you boy, one to remember as long as you live". An event to remember for sure, even if not for long. I remember thinking about that for when I reach the pearly gates I'd have to give an account of why I shot that snake that bit me. But I reckoned that snakes were around in Jesus' time too and I'll bet he would have had to have thrown a rock at one in his day. Bet if he'd a had my dad's .22 he'd a been as good a shot as me. Then I wondered if he had a dog as a boy growing up where he did. I wondered if it would have been a dog like old Spud. Jesus with a dog, a dog like old Spud. I knew my mind was going then. The sun was still a blazing and the water still felt good, but old Spud wasn't anywhere in sight. I guess he figured I didn't need him so we had wandered off somewhere on another adventure.

Seemed like hours later I was almost asleep when Tommy Taylor's dad came driving like a madman down the canal road. Tommy, and I played ball together at school. We weren't buddies or anything just kids that went to school together. Spud was raising hell barking and jumping near me so Mr. Taylor could see us. Spud knew I was in trouble, even more than I did at the time. Mr. Taylor worked for the Water Users Association and was always out checking gates up and down the canal. Old Spud had gone down the canal and found him. Reckon it was just like an old Lassie show where Lassie brings help to Timmy, who was always getting in trouble. As Mr. Taylor rolled up he was yelling at me and asking if everything was alright. I suppose the fact that I wasn't my talkative self gave me away. He could tell something was up cause I didn't get up.

My leg was really swollen up now and I didn't think I could get my boot back on. He looked at my leg and almost had a fit about me doing nothing but sitting there waiting to die. He took my knife from me and opened up the punctures which really felt pretty good to relieve the pressure from the swelling. Then he loaded me up in the back of his pickup and headed for the hospital up on 24th Street and Avenue A. On the way, I guess I was rambling on to Mr. Talyor about Spud, Jesus, floats on Main Street, and stuff that really made no sense because he later told me about my ramblings.

I must have been tired cause I was out like a light long before we ever got to the hospital. Spud must have been concerned too cause he was barking at me right up in my face to get me to wake up, but I didn't.

I lost the most part of that day and the next four days as well, cause I don't remember anything except the cold of the ice they had my leg wrapped in. I finally came around and they asked me what kind of snake bit me. I told them it was a Sidewinder, but they wouldn't believe me cause the wound was too deep and the marks so wide. They even sent my boot and sock to the resident expert hoping to get some venom extracted from the holes in the leather and cloth where the snake had bit through to my leg. They said they had to cut my belt off my leg and I reckon my tourniquet worked almost too good.

I was told later it was hit or miss that I would come out of this one. I had a good chance of cashing in my chips over a snake bite. Mom spent the better part of her days and nights with me praying that Jesus, would spare me from going to heaven. She felt sure I'd go to heaven if I died and said I'd catch Hell if I lived. She was hanging onto my hand so hard at times I thought she would cause me to lose my fingers.

They had moved me by ambulance that first day to Phoenix, where they had a major trauma center for snake bites. Dad said old Spud stayed in my room at home and wouldn't eat or drink at all till I was awake and speaking. They wouldn't have allowed that mangy mutt there with me in the hospital anyway so they didn't take him to Phoenix. Would have been his only trip outside of Yuma in his entire life you know. After a couple of days, I told them about the snake and where it happened. They wanted Dad to go find the snake if he could, so he took old Spud back out to the mesa where I said I was, and Spud took him to the old stump where I had left the rifle and my canteen. Dad said he found the snake and took it to the doctors at the hospital there in Yuma for them to examine. The head was still pretty much intact as I only shot the thing once at close range. Hell, Spud could of shot him too at that close a distance. I was getting pretty good with that old .22 rifle of Dad's, shooting snakes, cans, bottles, and such.

It was a Sidewinder alright, and a big one at that. They said it would be a record for size at 56 inches long, and if I lived I would be a record also at 13 years young. I got to keep my leg which allowed me to go to war some years later and be a hero, but that's a story that is to be told another time. They were worried it was a Mohave Rattler, I've seen them before and have shot a few in my time. To this day there is no anti-venom for the Mohave Rattle Snake. Those are the green glistening ones I've seen out toward Black Mountain, south of Florence, East off the main highway on Tom Mix Wash Road. The place is called 96 Ranch where they are so thick. But that's another story too and one I'll tell some other day.

When I finally got to come home, Mom said I had lost weight. I was always a skinny kid so I don't know how she would know that. One thing is for sure, hospital food sure don't do a body good. Spud was excited for me to get back home and we looked forward to going hunting again out on the desert just like we always did. For some strange reason, Mom got Dad in on the deal and they both said no more hunting. No matter what I said they were dead set against me going out looking for something to kill. My older brother Billy was even nice to me after the snake bite incident. Never really knew why he was different, but I think Mom made him be nice.

I got better at walking again after several weeks and me and old Spud went to see Mr. Taylor and to thank him for his help that day. He told me an extraordinary story about a shaggy old dog that came barking and raising hell up to where he was opening a canal gate. He could tell the dog was excited about something and wanted him to follow him. He said the dog ran down the canal bank at full speed for a long time till he got to where I was. Must have been 5 miles or so from where he started following him. "How that dog knew where I was working was a mystery", said Mr. Taylor, "and how he got me to follow him is even more of a mystery". Seems Mr. Taylor had seen an episode or two of Lassie in his day also. Said he knew right away I was in trouble when he saw my leg. Lucky thing that old dog was with me, or I wouldn't be writing this story now.

I loved that old dog long before anyone knew why. I can't say I loved him more after the snake bite, but I sure didn't love him less. That dog was my life for many of the years of my life growing up in Yuma. We were inseparable day and night except for school and church. Mom said he was the only one that knew me and either I was thinking like a dog or he was thinking like a human.

Many times I have thought about that snake bite incident and I believe it will be one of those things that does pass before my eyes in the end if anything does. Some years later old Spud had to be put down and I swear it broke my heart. I buried Spud down in the shade of the cottonwood trees along the canal bank where we loved to go. I go back to that spot from time to time and just sit and think about those times.

Dad said that old dog had just been on loan to me from wherever they come from, and had to go back there after his time was done here with us. I have had a lot of dogs in my life but never another dog like old Spud.

I will always remember Spud, wet, muddy, and standing proud to be up on that silly float in a grand parade right down main street. I owe that dog my life. Mom said, Jesus made that dog to watch over me, and that's a real good reason to Thank the Lord for Old Spud. ..... and I would have to say that's reason enough.

Bingo

5 or 6 Years Old

I never knew him by any name other than McKinney. He lived somewhere near the firehouse where my father worked as a city Fireman. McKinney was a retired fireman and would come to the firehouse to be with the men there to drink coffee and just hang out. McKinney had an old shaggy dog named Bingo. Anywhere McKinney went, Bingo would go also. But I'm ahead of myself in this recollection, so let me start back at the beginning.

I was about 5 or 6 years old when I first realized my father was only home every other day. He was a fireman for the city and worked those fireman hours: 24 hours on duty and 24 hours off duty. On many occasions, my mother would go to the firehouse to see my father and of course, I was with her when she did. Most times, as was the case in those days, visitors were not uncommon to the men at the firehouse. One of the most common visitors to that firehouse was a man known to me as McKinney and his dog Bingo. McKinney was actually Bill McKinney, a retired fireman from many years earlier and in a town I don't recall. Everyone called him McKinney, and I did also not meaning any disrespect at all. McKinney was his name and that was that.

McKinney lived a short walk from the firehouse and made it common practice to stop by to see the men on the different shifts and talk about news and calls the men had been on. I'm pretty sure McKinney never married as he never mentioned a wife. Having only his dog Bingo for companionship it seemed natural that seeing the men at the firehouse was a big part of his social calendar. McKinney was an older man and very slow in his walk and his speech. Bingo also was older and didn't run and jump with me as I'm sure he would have at a younger age.

Walking Bingo was a job I really liked 'cause me and Bingo got along just great. Bingo was not a small dog and would take up a lot of floor space in the little firehouse office where the men would sit and watch TV or just talk. Bingo liked me and would go where I would lead him and the guys liked me taking him outside anytime I was there. Bingo was sure that I had a treat for him as he always checked my pockets for anything I might have in the way of food. Many times he would be tired and wanted to lay down and sleep. So I would lay down with him and sleep also. We had a bond for sure. Sometimes we would roll around in the grass at the station house and I would get my clothes dirty as a result, which made my mother less than happy. But me and Bingo were fast friends and I loved him no matter what we did.

Oftentimes, the wives of the men on duty would stop by with a dish of some sort or another for all the guys. My mother made many things to drop by the firehouse for the men to enjoy and one of her best dishes was tuna casserole. McKinney was always invited to eat with the guys, and of course, he didn't eat much so he was not cutting into anyone's meal. McKinney just loved my mother's tuna casserole. It really was good but I do believe he was just being the nice guy he always was to everyone. McKinney was well-liked by all and always welcome when he and Bingo came by for a visit.

I might have been 10 years old when I started noticing McKinney was not at the firehouse when my mother and I went by to see my father. Dad said McKinney was not doing as good as before and didn't get out of his place much, as walking had become very difficult for him. I asked about Bingo and Dad said he would show up now and then for a handout at the firehouse but not much lately. The guys would stop by to check up on McKinney almost every other day to make sure he had food and see if there was anything they could do for him. The wives along with my mother made sure he had something to eat at his place. So began the tradition of cooking McKinney a special dish, along with a small pie or cake. Mom would drop it off at his small place around the corner from the firehouse. I would walk over to McKinney's place and do little chores for him and Bingo like picking up poop and making sure water was in the dish for my friend. I'd talk to Bingo and spend time with him as best I could.

I guess the days of my youth went by without my knowing about McKinney and Bingo getting older. It had been a while since I had seen them so I told my father I was going over to see how McKinney and Bingo were. He said not to go as they were gone. I asked what he meant by "gone." Seems both McKinney and Bingo died on the same day at his house just around the block several weeks before. I knew they were both old and that time was not on their side but did not think they would leave. My father thought it best not to tell me right away as he was not sure how I would handle it. As a 10-year-old boy, the death of people was not something I understood fully, but I felt the loss of my good friend Bingo more. I'd say the loss was medium hard for me to deal with.

My father said McKinney and Bingo went to Heaven together because they just couldn't live apart. They had always been together, and they would stay that way even now. Dad said the funeral was very nice, just a few of the guys were there, and that McKinney and Bingo were buried together. I think I felt better about them being gone when he told me that. Since that time I have always believed that all dogs go to Heaven. I know I'm right cause McKinney and Bingo are there right now together and that's the way it's supposed to be.

Seems like in no time at all my father brought home a mangy mutt for me to have as my own. Black and white medium-sized dog who my father said already had a name: Spud. I guessed him to be about a year or two old and we were the best of friends from the start. I often thought about Bingo when I was with Spud. I knew the day would come when Spud would leave me just like Bingo did.

As the years passed, we both got older and Spud got tired and didn't move as well as he did before. Turns out old Spud was older than I had thought he was. Then came the day Spud wouldn't or couldn't get up at all. The time had come for him to leave. I was heartbroken at the thought of my best pal going away without me to be with him. I remembered McKinney and Bingo were already in heaven, so I told Spud where he was going and that my friends were already there. I told Spud not to worry—my friend Bingo was there and he'd show him around the place right away. I asked my father if he remembered telling me that and he said that was a fact.

I don't know any more about the afterlife than anyone else. What I do know for sure and for certain is that Spud and Bingo will be waiting for me right inside the gate when I get to heaven.

Saying Goodbye to Gramps

I remember calling home one afternoon while away in the Navy to check up on Mom and Dad, the year was 1966. Grandpa was living with them at that time and if possible, I wanted to talk to him too. Mom said everything was fine and that it sure was good to hear from me. Spoke to her for a bit and she told me Grandpa was a real handful to deal with lately. I asked if Grandpa was able to come to the phone. She said she would go get him and I waited for him. Grandpa sounded different to me as he spoke. He seemed a bit distant in his speech, but I could still hear him.

"Hi Gramps, this is Bruce, how ya doing?"

"A lot better now that I'm talking to you. Listen to what I have to say and don't speak. I'm getting ready to go on a long trip. A trip I been planning to take for some time. I'm going alone and I'll be gone a long, long time. I'm tired more than ever and getting up every morning out-a bed just ain't worth it. "

"Gramps, are you going to visit relatives? "

"You bet I am, a whole bunch of 'em that I ain't seen now for many a year. We have had a lot of fun together since I got to know ya. Never knew you were coming along when you did. Times were good and watching you grow was fun for me. That time has come to an end, you need to go on and live your life. I just wanted you to know that I love you and that we really had some great times together along the way. Most of all I wanted you to know that I consider you to be my best friend. Goodbye boy, take care of yourself. I'll see you again one day. "

Mom came back on the phone and asked if I had a nice talk with Grandpa, she didn't hear any of the conversation at all. I remember to this day the way Grandpa talked and the clearness of his voice.

I had gone from child to adult some time ago but I had left the door open along my journey for fear of losing those wonderful times forever. What I did not realize was that I was still passing from childhood to adulthood and that

Grandpa was going to make that journey permanent by closing the door on my childhood.

It was two days later that I got word Grandpa was in the hospital and not doing well at all. Emergency leave was granted and I caught a flight home to see him if I could before he got worse or heaven forbid died.

I got home in the middle of the night and went right away with Dad up to see Gramps, in my Navy Uniform. When I got there he was sleeping. I held his hand and told him I was there. After several minutes Gramps opened his eyes and looked at me. His voice was soft and easy as he said

"Hey boy, you come to see me off?"

I recalled his words as he used to chase me around the yard down home in Yuma and I said

"Where you going in such a hurry?"

"Going on my last trip boy, got all I need."

"I don't want you to go just yet. Get better and we can get on with our time together. Soon as I get back from the Navy."

"I ain't got any time left in me, boy. Been figuring for ya. I was 68 when you was born, an I got to spend 20 years with you. That's a lot of learning we got done together, sure been fun."

Grandpa then gripped my hand real firm, and while looking deep into my eyes said, " Live your life full as you can, go for whatever you want, and it will be yours. Keep Jesus close to you always. Find a mate you can love with all your heart and make sure she is one you can trust with your life. Love you boy. "

Gramps then closed his eyes and within minutes he was gone. The door I had talked about was closed, never to be opened again.

I attended Gramp's funeral and cried a lot. Didn't have words to say anything to anyone. That marked the end of childhood for me.

I have attended many Adult Bible Study Groups over the years, and in several of them, the question was posed, "Other than Jesus, who do you want most to meet in heaven and spend time with? " Most people pick names right out of the Bible like John, or Paul, or Peter. I have never had to give that question any thought at all. I want to see my Gramps.

After the funeral, I spent some time going over the tools in the old shed where he used to putter. Everything that I could see was old, well-used, and some broken. Tools that were of importance to him, and cared for as if to be used at any moment. Blades on those that would cut were honed to perfection with a light coat of oil on them to keep them from rusting. A very large scythe stood in the corner of the shed ready as it were to give grass and weed a cut right down to the ground. All manner of woodworking tools hung and laid around the place. I would suspect that in the right hands, an entire home could be built with never a need for other tools. As I held and moved the tools I felt his hands in mine and seemed to know his touch just by the feel of the wood and metal. Old cans of varnish and paint were on shelves that I could see and the smell of them was almost overwhelming. An old cook stem pipe lay in an ashtray on the workbench. It contained the half-smoked remnants of tobacco that he used, and as I looked I saw it sitting on the top of the workbench backboard. A can of Prince Albert Smoking Tobacco, along with a small leather pouch filled with the same. The floor in the shed was dirt and the marks left there were smoothed over and over by the movements of his large boots with the laces dragging as he would shuffle along. A large man but stooped in stance from the years of hard labor that had made him that way. Old slouch hat on his bald head and thick glasses tinted green as I recall to keep the desert sun from blinding him. Always busy with one project or another in his shed. The heat of the summers in Yuma did not deter him from his work. Some task or another was always at hand and he would go about doing things at a pace that would seem to be in slow motion, but he would get one thing done and then move on to the next. As a boy, I would follow him around and wonder at his seemingly never-ending work. When I would ask a question of him he would stop and look at me for the longest time, and then either ignore me or answer with a soft-spoken voice that always gave specific detail to me so I would understand. I believe it was in him to speak in a way that was understood and not questioned by the listener, even if only six or seven years old.

I quickly learned not to run my fingers on blades that he had laying around, no matter how old or dull they might appear. They were never dull and they certainly were sharp as a razor, if they were meant to be that way. That old man never allowed any metal with a blade to be in his shed without a proper edge being on it at all times. I remember my dad taking things that needed to be sharpened to Granddad for that reason. I have often thought he did that just to give Grandpa something to do but realized after many years of working with metal edges that something's are learned only after many trials and errors.

I will always miss my Grandpa. I think I understood him more than any other man on this earth. He was gentle yet strong and gave me every chance to learn and grow some in his footsteps. I hope I can be like him in the many ways he showed me how to live. Thanks, Grandpa I Love You.

Rain on the Desert

Standing alone at a roadside rest stop on Interstate 8 halfway between Gila Bend and Yuma, Arizona, it occurred to me, I am where I belong in this world. At this age in my life living on the Great Southwest Desert is life as no other life anywhere on this planet I stood there watching the rain from the distant hills cover the ground, and I knew it was all well with me and my God. The clouds in my sight were so low and thick I could actually reach out and touch them and feel his shroud against my skin.

The Sun was still up there somewhere but not visible at all as the rain clouds took center stage. The smell of the rain on the desert mixed with a hint of sage and greasewood is so crisp and clean that nothing else can take its place. It puts Thanksgiving Turkey fresh out of the oven and Mom's Hot Apple Pie in the back seat of all things good and meaningful in this world. This place in this space and time, is the closest I will ever come to heaven here on earth. I know I must leave and move on down the highway to my destination, but I am torn between staying and going.

Eventually, I will have to go for I know this place and this feeling will go with me and I can recall it anytime I want to. This calm and peaceful feeling stays just beyond my senses, and I can go there when I need to get away. There I find that special magical destination in my heart and soul that gives me tranquility and the reason for my sanity if there is any in this crazy world. Headed for a funeral in Yuma, not a thing I looked forward to.

Riding My Dreams

Nobody

As a boy growing up in a small town, I wanted to be a lot of things. A happy man never really was part of those dreams. I thought as long as you were something, then happiness would be yours. Something or nothing is all I thought about. Something would be what everybody else was, and nothing would be what nobody was.

The more time I spent on this subject the more I realized I wanted to be a nobody. Nobody could do anything he wanted to cause he wasn't locked into being somebody like everyone else.

Once I had my mind made up I started off to become nobody. The first step to being a nobody was to become a paperboy. Nobody knows their paperboy. He is just the nobody that throws the papers they have ordered (so they can be somebody) in their yard as he rides by on his bicycle. He never reads what he delivers 'cause that would tend to make him a somebody.

Even when he comes to your house once a month to collect the paper bill he is really a nobody. Yuma Daily Sun for $.75 a week or $2.00 a month-- not a bad deal to learn all you needed to know to be somebody. Even Mary Ann Palmer didn't know who I was when I came to her house to collect the monthly bill so her parents could be somebody. She was somebody to me and I noticed right away that she would go far in this world if only on looks. She was absolutely gorgeous and had started growing those things that girls grow that boys notice even at that young age. She was always nice to me and I thought we had a connection once upon a time. Guess I was daydreaming cause it turns out I was just the perfect nobody to her.

Then I had an original thought. I would buy a crystal radio set and listen to late-night radio out of Texas or Oklahoma. So I got me one and put it together. It had one earpiece listening device but I could hear just fine back then with both ears. Man, that was the greatest.

Each night I would tune in to some show on the airwaves and listen to the music of the day. I really was a nobody then cause nobody listened to the radio in the middle of the night, I thought. And look at me, something I could do all by myself. We lived in a brick house and the reception wasn't good, so one night I went outside with my radio set and the reception was 10 times better. Mom got mad at me for being up past bedtime and for listening to God knows what on that radio set and she took it away from me. I remember her saying you must think you're somebody to do that sort of thing. She got me to wondering if maybe I was turning into a somebody.

Used to borrow my dad's .22 rifle and go out on the desert shooting. Living in Yuma, the summer days would get well over 100 degrees but I didn't mind that a bit. I'd go out on the desert a mile or two from the house and hunt snakes and rabbits. Long as I kept the rifle clean for Dad to use I could use it anytime I wanted. I figured nobody goes out on the desert in Yuma in the middle of the day, so I was being what I always wanted to be.

Always had a natural eye, as my dad would say, to shoot things dead center every time. Never feared getting bit by no snake cause I could see for miles in all directions at once so it seemed. Nobody could do that. I told my brother Billy once that I could shoot real good and told him I always hit the snakes in the head. He told me that's because snakes have such keen eyesight they can look right down the barrel of the gun when you point it at them and see the bullet coming. He said they are so fast that they actually strike at the bullet as it nears them, so even if I was a bad shot I would get my fair share of headshots too. He was my older brother and stood there lying to me as big as he pleased. I guess he thought I was a nobody and it didn't matter if he lied to me. I guess I didn't care about it myself cause I was truly becoming a nobody.

Mom would wash clothes every day to keep my dad in clean uniforms as an automobile mechanic. She made her own soap in a large galvanized tub in the backyard. She called it lye soap, and it was the only thing in the world that would clean my father's greasy, oily clothes. My clothes were hand-me-downs all my life and already somewhat threadbare. Just the clothes a nobody like me would wear, but clean from that lye soap.

Hair was another thing that I should mention. My father believed that boys don't need hair while growing up. High and tight was his motto and he owned the clippers in our house. So I was a real nobody in clean, ironed, faded-out clothes and no hair till I was out of high school. Took on the task of working for extra money to spend, by cleaning up backyards and throwing out trash for people.

While cleaning up the backyard of old Mr. Webster, a man that went to our church, I found something of interest. It was wrapped in burlap bags and wired up tight like a mummy or something that could get away if not treated in such a manner. Mr. Webster said it was of no importance to him and that I should just throw it out with the other unwanted junk from bygone years. I had to know what it was like for any boy my age and what I found when I unwrapped it was breathtaking. It was a 1946 Matchless 750 cc 1 cylinder Motorcycle with the chain missing, and no wheels or tires. It was beautiful, like nothing I had ever seen before. It had a little brass plaque stuck on the gas tank reading: Track Record Salinas, California - 1950 - 1951 * 98 MPH *

I asked if I could have the motorcycle since he was going to throw it out anyway, and he looked at me like I was crazy or something. "Boy, this is the machine that took my brother from me. Hell, this machine is a killer and it sure isn't for children to be playing with, even if it never will run again. Just you throw it out and forget about it."

I told him I would take it in pay for my work and I would even clean out his shed and straighten up everything for it. He looked at me for a long time, then at the motorcycle.

"I know of two other people that died riding that God-forsaken machine. As sure as I'm standing here, it will kill you, too. But if you think you can get it started and ride it without going to meet your maker, you're welcome to it. Just swear you will never try racing it."

I swore that I wouldn't and thought I had the better end of this bargain. Nobody had one of these, I thought, and away I went dragging it home, much to my father's dismay. I tried real hard to get it running. Engine came apart easily enough and I could tell even with limited ability that the rings were shot, therefore I could get no compression when trying to start it.

Dad looked it over and decided DeSoto rings of that size would work. So I bought a set and put the thing back together with a new gasket here and new tapped-and-threaded bolt there, hoping it would start, but secretly praying it wouldn't. I did not want any part of going 90-plus miles an hour on this old beast with very little in the way of brakes. But then brakes wouldn't make it run, so I thought one thing at a time and put brakes at the end of my fix-it list.

I figured that a somebody wouldn't even try to fix this old relic, but a nobody like me was perfect for the job. Cleaned out and reset the carburetor. Adjusted the old magneto, drained and refilled the crankcase and transmission. Then came the clutch and all I could do was clean it, sand it up a bit, and hope it would work.

Then with everything ready I gave her a stomp with the old kicker. I remember yelling as the beast roared to life "Holy Shit!". Run it did and very well for an old hunk of metal that had been wrapped up in captivity for some 15-odd years, and I could tell I had a handful with this machine. Time after time it fired right up and ran like it was brand new and breathing fresh air for the first time after being bound and gagged for all those years.

Now all I really needed were tires, wheels, and a chain to make her go. I also needed brakes to make her stop, but that was still at the end of my list. My dad was just as interested in getting the thing going as I was, being a motorcycle rider in his youth.

Took a while but soon the bike was together and ready to ride. I had Harley-Davidson wheels and tires with a new chain and drive sprockets. Dad was taking no chances and took me out into the desert on the hard pack to ride the machine, away from everyone and everything. Said if I killed myself he would bury me right there on the spot and bring Mom by on my birthday to visit. Fitting for a nobody, I thought, and it just might happen.

I had no choice in the matter, you know. Men, and boys too, put themselves into situations like this without thinking sometimes. It's a macho thing we do to earn the passage to manhood. I wanted to be a man even if a nobody type of man.

So with an old army helmet, I had found and a beat-up pair of welding goggles, I fired up the machine and sat on it while it warmed up. A slight adjustment to the fuel mixture and I was ready to ride. With clutch in, I stomped it into first gear and got ready to go. I looked at my dad with one last look. You might know the look I'm talking about. The look that says, "I don't really want to do this. but if you're not going to stop me then I'll have to do it." He didn't do or say a thing and the silence from him was almost louder than the motorcycle.

I still remember that feeling as the bike took off and I was hanging on with every bit of strength that I could muster. The hand throttle went to full open and stuck in that position, which is something I had not counted on. Here is where I mention the two points about speed. One is fast and can take some time to achieve. The other is quick which takes no time at all to achieve. I had never been to 90-plus miles per hour in my short life, not ever, never, and certainly not as quick as that machine between my shaky legs was taking me there. We were absolutely flying and I was on my way to the ride of a lifetime for sure, and having bought my ticket to ride, I was going to stick it out.

I swear death was approaching me as fast as I was approaching the horizon. That little brass plaque kept running through my mind about the 98 miles per hour record in Salinas, California, the three dead riders that went before me, and the everlasting reminder of how brakes should not be last on anyone's list of needed parts. The brakes didn't work and the clutch would not disengage. The increase in speed was happening faster than I could handle and, even with goggles firmly in place, I was losing my ability to focus.

Then I had a brainstorm. I reached down and pulled the fuel line from the gas tank and held the clutch in for all I was worth. I swear it took what seemed like a lifetime, but it died for lack of fuel and finally came to a stop, after covering the other half of Yuma County. I got off of that silent machine and laid it down none too gingerly, walked several steps, and collapsed on the ground near it, but not so close that it could touch me. Dad came up in the truck to where I was. It took him a while mind you. I must have covered 5 miles. He said, " Damn Boy that thing is a Rocket ". I looked at him and said, "I want to go home."

We loaded up the bike in the truck and drove back home. Dad never said a word all the way there. I didn't mind, I had some thinking to do. I needed to evaluate my decision to be a nobody. Dad made the adjustment to the throttle so it would work right. Fixed the fuel line and made a couple of adjustments here and there and fixed the brakes. He rode the bike several times around the block and back and forth to work, and told me the bike ran just fine.

That's as close to dying as I had come to in my young life. I saw the face of death and had lived to tell the tale. I knew that machine was going to kill me if ever I rode it again. I looked at it many times after that but never did ride it again.

I recounted the event to the man who gave me the machine, and he went into his story of how it had killed this guy and had mangled that guy and so on. Said that motorcycle is the cause of at least three deaths that he knew of. He looked me straight in the eye and said, "Son, you are a very lucky boy."

I really knew for certain that death could be cheated. There would be others in years to come. I have had other motorcycles in my life and I was a Motorcycle Policeman for a number of years. Riding motorcycles for pay was easy and challenging with all the right training. Riding them for fun and pleasure is exciting if you know what you are doing. Riding them because you want to prove you are a man or nobody for that matter, is stupid and childish, especially if you have never done it before. My dad knew that but it was something I had to learn. Some things in life are like that. That old motorcycle and the ride it gave me changed my thinking. To be somebody wasn't a bad thing, and happiness does come with it if you put in the effort required. To be a nobody takes a lot of work and most of it amounts to nothing. I figured I was just too lazy for that.

At 14 years old I figured something out that I had been working on for some time. You know, it felt pretty good. Hell, I might even turn out to be somebody - if I can live long enough.

Being There

Mom called and I drove to Yuma to be with Dad one last time. It was February 2001 and Dad had been bedridden for several weeks in a hospital bed Hospice provided for his use at home. I remember getting to the house in the early morning hours around 2:30 am or so and Mom telling me his breathing was labored and he was going to go soon. I held Dad's hand and told him I loved him. I thanked him for everything he did for our family. For always providing and for keeping us safe through the years. I hugged him and let him sleep. I was tired from being up so long so I went to sleep around 7:30 am. Mom sat with Dad the rest of the morning and on into the day. She said he woke up at around 10:00 am and asked if I was there, she told him yes, and he said he wanted the prize. She knew what that was and went and got my Rodeo Buckle out of the drawer. When she returned to him he was asleep again. At about noon she woke me to tell me Dad had passed away in his sleep. His body was still warm when I went to him. He would have been 83 years old in May 2001. The hurt I felt at that time was not so much for Dad but for Mom. Mom was now alone and had to live on without her life partner. She gave me the buckle he had held so dear all those years past. She told me he wasn't gone, he was just gone on ahead to be with his Lord.

I drove home on a desert night mom said it was his time
at daybreak, we were together the words were hard to find
I sat beside him where he lay his breathing was very faint
color of his skin had left he was as pale as old dried paint
I had so much to say and I knew he'd understand
I felt him tighten his grip as I held him by his hand
he opened his tired old eyes a dim light shined within
he knew I was his son that had grown to be his friend
Mom and I got on our knees and thanked him for the years
thanked him for the man he was with eyes so filled with tears
we prayed for peace from heaven be with us here below
we prayed to be forgiven we cried cause he had to go
in silence there as we gathered I felt at peace and calm

183

I knew my loving savior had my father in his arms
Thanks Dad Thanks for giving us your life.

Still on The Road

Once again on the road to Yuma to see Mom. Friday afternoon, got off early for the weekend and plan to spend the time at the old homestead with my mother. Been several weeks since I was down to see her. Work has been very heavy for me lately. I have been working doing compliance for UPS now for several months and it just keeps getting busier and busier.

Being a single guy with no commitments to anyone I can pretty much call the shots on my personal time. My girls are both grown and gone from me living their own lives, so no ties to them at all these days.

Mom had mentioned she needed some help moving some furniture so along with some yard work for her I am going to do the best I can in the time I have with her. Living alone as she does down-home since Dad passed in 2001, she has done very good for herself. Been 5 years now and she seems to be alright with the house and the friends she still has in town. She had to give up driving and I sold her car so she really does depend on her girlfriends to get around, shopping, doctor appointments, church, and everything else. Hope I can get all she needs for a while at the grocery store and anything else while I am there. Come Monday if we need to do more we will. because my job can just wait till I get back whenever that is.

Two in the afternoon and I'm making good time. Rolling into Gila Bend for a break and a bite to eat. No breakfast this morning as I was wanting to get to work early to file my reports for the week. That being done I left for my weekend and time down-home with Mom. Space Age Restaurant is always there for me to get something to eat and drink and relax a bit from the highway. Judy always seems to be there when I come in, and she knows where I'm headed for the weekend. Burger and fries with coffee no cream has already been ordered for me before I even sit down. She brings me the newspaper for the day out of Phoenix and we exchange greetings as always. Soon the talk will turn to her kids and how they are doing in school. I almost feel like a part of her extended family who comes to see her about every 6 weeks or so. Not too many people in the place at the hour I arrived, and that is really to my liking. Gives me time to talk to Judy.

Off again I go after my lunch break and the road stretches out before me like it always does. 118 miles from Gila Bend to Yuma on Interstate 8 and it never changes. My car is a 1996 Cadillac El Dorado and I sure do love its ride on the highway. Smooth and steady like a custom-built chariot for the long haul. It is always a long drive and for the most part, nothing to see.

As always my mind wanders to times that I have made this journey to Yuma from where I have lived in Tempe and Chandler over the years. With one woman, with her and one, then two girls. Alone as I am now and over the years with various other people that I lived with even married on occasion. It's amazing that I have lived this long and have one living older brother who is coming to Yuma as well this weekend to see Mom. Kinda like a family reunion of sorts, even if only three of us left.

Billy had a stroke some time back but still gets around in his car and makes the drive from his home in Lake Havasu, to see Mom about every other month or so. It's always great to get together with my family and talk about what is going on in their lives. We always get to go to a restaurant in town for lunch and it is usually a favorite buffet where each of us can pick what we want to eat. Mom never has much and Billy and I can have something different every time. The place was a favorite of Dad's also and Mom likes it because he did. After lunch, we go shopping for Mom and stock her up with groceries to last till the next time we come to see her.

Sunday morning we all go to Mom's church with her and meet and greet people there that we have come to know over the years. Always good to sit with Mom in church again as I did all those years growing up in Yuma. Mom always wants me and Billy to meet her friends and she always introduces us as if it were the first time we were to meet them. The pastor is always glad to see us and always has a word or two about Mom. Time for the Sunday Noon meal and we go to IHOP for pancakes which is a fatal flaw with us for Sunday Brunch time. Sunday afternoon Billy has to leave to drive home and we all hug and say goodbye. I too have done all I can for Mom this trip. Furniture got moved, some things got thrown out, some things rearranged in the cupboards, and bathrooms cleaned as is always on my to-do list. It's now time for me to turn my car towards home up in Chandler, Arizona a drive of 183 miles to get there. On the road sometimes I would again stop in Gila Bend on my trek, sometimes not. As good as it always was to get home and off the highway, I never was in a hurry to end the day. My memories of being with the ones I love are always with me and carry me on in this life so I never have to hurry away from them. Besides when I do get home my attention always turns to ironing and getting my clothes ready for another week

On this particular Sunday afternoon, I found myself driving in a dark and cloudy time on the highway. Stopping in at one of the rest stops along the highway I used the facility and then just stood out in the open watching the rain clouds move off in the distance. Once again I could smell the rain and knew it was headed my way. After a long pause just watching and smelling the rain, I dove on towards home. The rain did not ever overtake me on the road and I made it home without so much as a sprinkle on the windshield. Alone at home, I was never really alone for I had the times I got to spend with family again.

As was always my way, I called Mom to tell her I made it home safe and sound, and to tell her how great it was to see her again and to see Billy as well. I told her I'd call her again toward the end of the coming week to check on her and told her I loved her.

This story was a dream I had the other night here in Prescott, where I now live with my wife of 11 years. Mom could no longer stay by herself in 2006 and I moved her to my town of Chandler, Arizona, and into an assisted living home.

Mom never was willing to live with me in my house, she was just that independent. For seven years and several moves of homes, Mom made it through with flying colors.

Mom passed away in 2014 the same year me and Georgia moved up to Prescott. It's now 2019 and even after 5 years the memories of the drive to see Mom and Billy are as clear as if it was today.

I trust that my mind will remain clear for many years to come so I can relive these times with them. Being on that long lonely highway was never one of my favorite things to do, but it did have happy memories as a result of enduring it over and over again. Of course, Gila Bend and Judy are part of those times.

That Door

She was asleep when I arrived. I could see her sitting in her easy chair just inside the front window. I knew the door would be open for me as she knew I was on my way. I could hear Christmas Music playing low from the radio she always had beside her chair. I just stood there before opening that door for a moment and the memories of so many years flooded my mind with visions of bygone days. I really didn't want to disturb her sleep, cause I knew she would be dreaming of Dad, her partner in life for 56 years. When we speak she tells me how lonely she is without him. Dad passed away some four years ago now. It's 2005 and it doesn't seem to get any easier for her. Living in the same house since 1951 gives a body roots and a degree of comfort in the same place with the same walls. She raised three boys in this house and it wouldn't be natural to say there wasn't a window or two broken along the way, cause there certainly were. The paint has changed over the years. Trees and shrubs have come and gone mostly not able to take the harsh climate in Yuma, Arizona. Dogs, cats, and animals of all sorts were part of growing up there. Furniture too has come and gone, but one thing has always been the same since the house was built; that door

I started thinking about the many times I had come to this door over my lifetime. Sometimes alone, sometimes with a girlfriend or wife. Even my own children have passed through that door many times with me. I just don't think they understand the meaning that door has had for me all these years. The times I have come here and found Mom and Dad waiting to greet me and welcome me home and invite me to pass through that door.

I remember as a kid watching the wind outside knowing I was safe behind that door. Inside this house as a child I would look out the window to see the wind move the sand. Outside the wind would blind the onlooker but behind glass, I could watch the magic. The wind would take the sand and throw it against anything and everything. The sand didn't seem to care as it knew no amount of anger the wind could send would hurt it. From my safe vantage point, I could watch the dance of the sand and the wind. I knew it would never change and I could come back, again and again, to see the rivals moving in tune with nature's song. The sand would pile up on our front porch and then be moved to another location as if the wind couldn't make up its mind where it wanted it. The wind didn't seem to mind me watching and the sand just moved on its way without a care about the boy in the window. The boy behind that door. I have often thought about the Wind and the Sand as my life moves as it does.

The similarities are amazing to think of. I truly feel like sand being blown about by the Wind as I move from place to place and person to person. I don't fear the Wind it is the force that drives us, much like the Sand. I don't know where I will be taken next but it's all in a plan I will one day know. But for now, I'm content to be standing at that door once again.

My mind then raced off to the time I dated a girl from our church. Her name was Susan, and she was a born-again Christian. The girl had an award-winning smile and a set of breasts that would turn any young man's head. Susan, and I found out about the birds and the bees in the front seat of Dad's 54' Chevy Truck. The night turned into dawn and both of us were naked as Blue Jays sitting there in the front seat of that old truck. Our clothes in a heap on the floorboard and as we looked at each other in the first light of day we found no shame in what we had done. It was beautiful and all the world around us was right and bright, and true.

I can't even say it was my idea to go all the way, but once having a taste of sex, we indulged as often as we could. Two good church-going kids hungry for what life had to offer. I remember bringing her to meet Mom and Dad as if to get their blessing or something. After meeting my folks I remember Susan saying she would like to marry a boy with folks like that one day. I stopped seeing Susan soon after that cause I was in the US Navy, and I don't know why I thought of her now.

I remember warm summer nights with the door open all night long, and how cool the air felt in the mornings flowing in slowly. The smell of fresh coffee brewing, and Dad's pipe tobacco burning. Seemed like that door was never closed much, certainly never locked.

Once I came home on leave from the Navy, and I was in uniform of course as all military had to travel in uniform. Dad met me at the Marine Base and shook my hand as we met. I wanted to hug the guy but it wasn't his way of doing things, and a handshake was the way he did things. He didn't say much on the ride home except to ask how long I would get to stay. Mom was in tears when I arrived and walked up to that door. I knew her tears were tears of joy, not sadness, and as I walked through that door the world I had known in the foreign place disappeared and I was home again. I thought mom would never stop hugging me and let me go but she finally did. Dad just looked at me and said he was glad to see I was well. He said war is hell and didn't ask about any of my ribbons I had pinned over my breast pocket. I was an E-4 at that time and had two more years to go, but I was ready to get out of the service and settle down back home. I wanted to start a business, I wanted to go to college, I wanted to get married, I wanted to be somebody— yeah I had a lot of I-want to's.

I knew my time at home was going to be short and that I would have to leave soon. I tried not to think about it and just live for the moment. I wondered where Susan, had gone off to, and if she still wanted a boy with folks like mine. Turns out she missed me as much as I missed her and we acted like the time we were apart never really happened. A girl like Susan could sure do a boy good at that time and place in his life. How she never got pregnant, or if so, never told me, is still a mystery. That was the last time I ever saw Susan.

I went to church with Mom, and of course wore my uniform, at her request, for all the world to see. I saw things differently then and heard the words of the sermon differently also. Somehow I knew something they didn't know. In that foreign place, people just like me were going to die today, and yet I was here with mom and I could smile through it all and shake hands with everyone. I had the distinct feeling that Jesus was not with us that day in church, but in that foreign place where I had left him.

The time went by very fast and it was time for me to leave. Once mom turned me loose, with tears streaming down her face like rain, I walked past that door again and thought maybe for the last time. Dad took me to the Marine Base to catch my flight out. As we parted we shook hands again and Dad said be sure to come home for your mother. He never said he loved me, nor did I speak those words to him. I told him I had been trained well and had the will to survive. He said that will have to do.

191

I have walked up to that door so many times over the years and never felt the way I feel right now. I have been tripped up and fallen many times in my life but I always found that door to be my sanctuary from whatever life had given me. It was always like being back at the beginning and I could start over here every time. I have found myself starting over many times and it's wonderful knowing you have a good starting point. The years have passed, I have loved different women, even married a few. My children have grown and moved on, and even now I find that the open door to this little house welcomes me in to find rest, peace, and calm.

I finally opened that door quietly and slipped into the house of my youth. I sat down in a chair across from Mom and watched her as she slept and I'm sure dreamed of Dad. I thought of many things that night but one thing was sure, I was home. I sat there till I too fell off to sleep. I felt secure in my heart that I had once more returned to the safest place on earth. I often wonder if when I die and heaven looms into view, there will be a door like this one there to welcome me home. I do know Mom and Dad will be there, my brothers, my friends, and my best friend as a boy, my dog Spud. Home for me will always be that place, that house, that door.

My Church

We left at 4:00 am and drove up the highway for three hours to the point north of Wikieup where we turned onto a dirt road for the area we were going to hunt. It was to be a four-day hunt for Javelina and we were wide-eyed to be getting there. We drove on a winding road through hills, mountains, and flat lands till we came at last to the camping area some 20 miles off the main highway. The day was one of perfect weather and the sun was bright as we arrived. It felt good to be there in this place where we knew we would have time to forget about the world back home and all the traffic and fast pace of work. The first thing that met us was the silence of everything and the sweet smell of sage on the light breeze as we stood in awe of what we beheld. I took in the landscape with sight, sound, and smell as if for the first time in my life and it was amazing. This place, I kept thinking, is where my God lives and he is here with me now showing me the wonders he has created. The air was crisp and clear, as were the rocks which had been washed clean from recent rains. Everywhere I looked I could see green, red, yellow, and blue as the Desert was alive and all the colors were vibrant in every hue visible to the human eye. I was in that place I have always known was in my heart and in the very soul of me. After several moments I walked up a small rise about 100 yards from where we would camp and found a wonder beyond my dreams. An open space cut out of the stone ridges and at the bottom of it a stream running slowly with water as pure as any on earth. My heart was full at that moment and I could not imagine being allowed to share this place in time. The water of life was there before me in this Desert place and as I tasted it I knew the hand of God was there. I thanked him for this perfect moment in my life

As I took this all in I was given a sense of peace like I had only known a few times in my time on the Desert. I then turned to see a rock rising up like a cathedral from the earth and could only see it as a place of majesty built for me to behold in reverence at its beauty. I then thought of the woman in my life who is with me always in my heart and wished she could be with me now at this moment in person to drink of this pure water and know as I do that he lives. With her, I could live in this place for all of my days. These things have been here since the beginning of time and will remain till the end of time. With her and these wonders, I would never want for another thing. With her, I believe I can be the person God wants me to be.

After several days in this place without being successful in our hunt we left to return to our lives back in the city. I was ready to leave and return to the world and I knew I had been allowed to view God's handiwork firsthand. That to me is the closest I have ever come to heaven here on earth. I want to take my woman to this place one day and share with her the Church I found on the Desert.

2014

Dad's on a great Golf Course, Mom's in a wondrous Kitchen, Grandpa is in a marvelous Metal Shop, and my brothers are outside playing. That's the way I remember them. As for me, I keep stumbling around here in this life. Looking for things to do to occupy myself as time moves along slowly. Remembering times and people and places is what I do. Seems to work for me to clear my mind and move me out of the haze of time.

The Story As Old As Me

It's December and in another 20 days, I'll be 76 years old. Hard to believe I am that age even with aches, pains, and lack of mobility, hearing, and eyesight.

I wanted to say that I never did tell my kids about how I grew up and what I did as a boy. They knew my folks and got to spend time with them over the years before they passed away. But they never really understood what I did and why I am the way I am because of it. I wish I had taken the time to explain to them the life and times of their dad in that distant place called Yuma. Never too late, as they say, to make it clear to those that don't know. For some reason, I feel the need to tell my story and I can only do that on paper and by giving it some careful thought.

Me as a boy, me as a man, my time in the US Navy, my first wife, her parents, my parents, other women, my work, and my life as I lived it is all rolled up in a great big ball. I will now try to lay it all out in a straight line so everyone can see what it was all about. I'm sure my daughters think it was just a fantasy and through it all, they appeared magically into this world without much fanfare. From my point of view, it was magic and they are main players in the show. This story will be mostly in first person but may go in and out of third person as I tell the story. The curtain rises and here we go.

December 25, 1946, at 10:00 am or so in Yuma, Arizona at General Hospital down on Avenue B, Annie Mae Watson Thompson Sparks, age 27, Sales Clerk, gave birth to a boy child and gave him the name of Bruce Darrell Sparks. I am told it was a cold day in Yuma and actually snowed according to my father Robert Burley Sparks. age 28, Auto Mechanic.

At the time of my birth, my family lived at 763 Orange Avenue in Yuma. An old home even then and made of Adobe with walls 14 inches thick. Very cool in the heat of summer and somewhat warm in the cold of winter. Not a big house with two bedrooms, one bath, a front room, and a kitchen. We had linoleum flooring over old wood planks that creaked and groaned a lot. I remember a fireplace in the kitchen area that we never used but was a great place for a boy to hide. I had two older half brothers from mom's previous

197

marriage to a man named Clyde Thompson, whom she had divorced in 1943 for non-support. Jimmie Marion and Billy Clyde were my brothers and they were older than I, Jimmie was born in 1939, and Billy was born in 1941

As I grew to the age of 5 years, my folks bought a house out on the Mesa at 824 Cactus Drive. The year was 1951 and Dad was now a Fireman for the City of Yuma. It was a great job for Dad and the family. Steady pay and work that was 24 hours on and 24 hours off so he was home every other day. Mom at that time began her studies at home to become a Nurse, which she completed and got her license, and went to work for a local doctor. Some years later she worked full-time at the Yuma Regional Hospital.

At the age of 10 years, I became interested in horses and in due time, with the encouragement of my brother Billy, I got into Little Britches Rodeo Events where ever they were held in and around Yuma and California.

It was the thing to do for a boy in Yuma where there was little interest in school and girls were not part of his world yet. The years between about 1956 to 1964 were all about my riding horses, my brother Billy, and dealing with those things as my main interest in growing up in Yuma. I have written those stories.

In 1964 I graduated from Kofa High School and that same year became 18 years old and too old to ride in Little Britches Events. It was that very year that Billy's horse Duke got hurt and he decided to give up Rodeo as his means of entertainment. Duke was sold, Billy moved to San Diego, and I joined the US Navy. We went in different directions initially for a while which turned into a lifetime of changes.

January 1965 I left Yuma on a midnight bus to the US Navy Bootcamp in San Diego, California. Three months later I was sent to Memphis, Tennessee for training in Aviation Electronics. After that, I went to North Island San Diego for more training, Moffett Field San Francisco for more training, and then to Barbers Point Hawaii to Patrol Squadron VP-28.

There I was assigned to Crew 7 as Electronic Julie Operator aboard a Lockheed Orion P-3. Second day at my new duty station I was on my way to Midway Island for 5 days of flights out over the Pacific flying 12 hours every day for those 5 days. After that, it was routine to go almost anywhere in the

Pacific including Vietnam, Australia, Japan, Canton, Johnson, Alaska, Okinawa, and the Philippines. By that time I was 19 years old I was learning to fly the very plane I was assigned to as an air crewman. All crewmen were schooled in flying the aircraft as a matter of emergency drill in case one of us had to take over for the Captain of the plane.

In October of 1966 VP-28 deployed to Adak, Alaska for 6 months, and I had never seen or felt cold like that until I got to that God Forsaken place. It was said that on Adak Island there was a woman behind every tree. There were no trees so that saying made perfect sense. The water temperature all around the island was 28* and did not melt because of movement and the salt content in the ocean. Adak is an island near the end of the Aleutian Island Chain of the Archipelago Southwest of Alaska. For some reason, I took comfort in knowing that the Air Force was on Shemya Island and it was further out than we were. Flying was the job and flying we did. In 180 days flying out of Adak, I logged well over 1500 flight hours, earned my Aircrew Wings, and made 2nd Class Petty Officer E-5 Aviation Anti Submarine Warfare Technician. Besides the Pilots job, I learned the third seat in the cockpit Aviation Maintenance Technician, Radio Operator, Navigator Assistant, Radar, Jezebel Operator, Electronics Counter Measures Technician, and Ordinance. From Adak, we flew to Seattle, Juneau, Fairbanks, Whidbey Island, Barrow, Vancouver, and Kodiak. Great to get to see so many of these places and get to spend time being there.

After Adak and back in Hawaii in 1967 things went along as my time was spent in training missions and flights and living the military life. In 1968

I met an Island girl that captivated my world and we were together every chance we got. Gwendolyn Toshiko Chinaka was her name. Her parents Ralph and Grace Chinaka accepted me as her boyfriend and we spent many hours together as a family getting to know one another. These people were of Japanese descent but as American as Apple Pie. I truly loved them. They took me with them to all the relatives get togethers and after learning who they were I was just another member of a large family. Military to them was as Hawaiian as the Sun that rose every day. January 10, 1969, I married Gwen in Hawaii and shipped out on January 20th for San Francisco, California to exit the US Navy having served my 4-year hitch. January 24th,

1969 Gwen met me at San Francisco Airport and we drove down the coast of California to Yuma, Arizona in my 1964 Volkswagen Beetle with no heater. It was Cold.

Took us two days to drive down to Yuma. I had one suitcase, Gwen had three and the little car was packed full. Needless to say, we were cold and tired from the trip. Arriving in Yuma was everything I had told her it would be, and my family accepted Gwen as if she was a long-lost child that needed more love and affection than anyone ever. The fact that she was pregnant was explained and accepted as well. We spent about a week there with the folks and then drove up to Tempe, Arizona where I planned to go to school at Arizona State University to seek a degree of some sort.

Together we found a sweet little apartment furnished, with no charge for water or electricity $100.00 a month and we took it and moved in right away.

This was February 1969 and I needed a job to support myself and the wife. I applied everywhere I could think of but no one was hiring. Then the City of Tempe had an opening and I went there and got a job at the Police Station. Started right away and we were off and running with income. Within a few months, we found the little one-bedroom cottage on Roosevelt Street owned by Mrs, McKinny. It was $50.00 a month including water and electricity, it was furnished, and I had to cut the grass and trim it as part of the deal. We took it just before Kelly was born. Gwen's parents bought us a washing machine, my parents bought us a dryer and we used cloth diapers for our little girl to save money over disposable diapers. We had a Cat named Rajah and I did most of the cooking because Gwen did not know how to cook. I was close to my work and could ride a bike or walk if need be, and that proved to be important.

Time passed, Kelly grew, and we soon bought a house in Tempe at 1911 E. Dunbar Street. Almost right behind the Gemco Store on Baseline Road. A small three bedroom, one and a half bathrooms, carport home with a fenced yard so we could have a dog. The house was just East of McClintock and just North of Baseline Road. Not long after moving in, we got Chance our Doberman, our family dog and companion for Kelly. The two of them were inseparable. I believe it was three years later when we moved again. This time to a larger house on Kenwood Lane between McClintock and Price just North of Guadalupe Road. It was a four-bedroom, two-bath house on a large cal de sack with six other homes.

I was attending community college with my eye on getting a degree in Criminal Justice. I did get my associate's degree and transferred to ASU to continue my studies.

My career with the Police Department in Tempe took on new and exciting roles for me. I was Motorcycle Officer and I loved the job. My college aspirations were coming true as I attended Mesa Community College to get an Associate's Degree, and Gwen went to ASU to finish up her Fine Arts Degree. In time I too went to ASU and all was going along just fine for our growing family as Autumn joined us in 1976. Cats, dogs, and whatever else were all part of our family over the years. We had great neighbors and

a wonderful neighborhood to live in. We even built a large swimming pool in our back yard which had room for two such pools. Life for us was wonderful and we held to very closely held family values. Trees, fencing landscape, remodels, patio cover, and we were set to grow even more.

Gwen expanded her business in Dog and Cat Grooming to a storefront not far from our home, and it was a tremendous success.

In May of 1977, Gwen told me of her desire for me to stop being a Police Officer as she did not hold with the lifestyle that came with it. Our relationship was on the line and after a good deal of discussion about it, I quit my job with Tempe Police Department. I had no job and no idea what I would do for income. But it was exciting again to have no way out of our needs and nowhere to go. I then found work at a Fish Store Skippers Island selling tropical fish and learning how to set up tank systems for Doctors and other professionals. It paid very well and we were again in the black with my earnings. After a few months, the store owner closed the business over a dispute with his wife and I was again out of work. So I started selling Motorcycles at Don Weeks Kawasaki in Mesa, Arizona. I had never been involved in the sales of a vehicle before, and it was fun and once again paid well, as it seemed everyone wanted a motorcycle. Then one day I talked to the United Parcel Service Driver as he was delivering to the motorcycle store and got interested in that kind of work. I was 31 years old and had the desire to do the work offered by UPS as a delivery driver and did that job for 12 years. Not being a Policeman saved the marriage between me and Gwen and we went on for another 8 years as a married couple with kids. When I quit the Police Department I also stopped attending college as the days at UPS were long and very tiring with no time at all for school. I left the pursuit of my degree with only a course or two left to go to earn the Bachelor's Degree. 30 years later I ended my career at UPS and again turned my attention to getting the degree at the insistence of a friend.

On New Year's Day in 1985, Gwen made her statement of disenchantment with our living arraignment stating the love was over, that she would be living elsewhere, and that a divorce was in order. I went into the classic 5 stages of this situation. Denial, Anger, Bargaining, Depression, and finally Acceptance. It took me three months to realize that Gwen had another man in her life and that he was her motivation to leave me and the kids. With that, firmly in my head I filed for divorce and got it in November of 1985. We split up stuff and arranged to have the kids 6 months a piece during the year. I stayed in the house with the agreement that if and when it sold she would get half of the proceeds from the sale. We had made it 16 years as man and wife and that was my part in the relationship. Her part was to grow away from me and the family that we had made together. Never saw that coming. Lots of hurt for me but all these years later I can truly say it worked out fine. I did not come out of the marriage without a great deal of damage to my view of life and women, but I seemed to be able to bounce back after several bad decisions and disastrous marriages that followed.

30 years with UPS was enough for me and they had planned to make the job difficult as their corporate way of making people retire. I did just that in April of 2007, I took the retirement package that they offered me and left the company. In 1999 while employed as the District Driver Trainer at UPS I met the woman that I would marry in 2008, but it was a very rocky relationship over those years. We worked together and then apart but stayed connected through the work I did. In 2007 she called me to see how I was doing in

retirement and we talked at length about what I would do with my life. She encouraged me to return to college to attain my Bachelor's Degree in Criminal Justice. It was not easy to return to the academic setting of college but I did it and got the degree to hang on my wall. All that was left for me in life to make it all worthwhile was to find a partner to share every day of living with.

It was 2007 and I was retired from UPS and doing a lot of hunting and fishing from my home in Chandler, Arizona. I had a dog at that time named Bugs, he was 5 years old and a very inquisitive male Pug. We went everywhere together mostly hunting and fishing as mentioned. That year the woman from UPS, Georgia, informed me she was leaving her husband and seeking a divorce from him. The handwriting was on the wall about us and we were destined to start being together. After introducing her to my kids, we dated till February 2008 and married. Small ceremony in the office of our pastor at that time with only four people as witnesses. Georgia had four kids from her previous marriage, and I was not accepted as their new stepfather right away. They did not feel that she had divorced their father but that she had divorced them, and I was the reason.

Georgia was what I wanted more than anything ever before, and I decided that I had married her, not her kids, it was not a package deal, therefore I didn't care what they thought. My two girls were more than open and loving with Georgia because they saw in her the perfect kind of woman for me and they grew to love her right away.

The years rolled on and Billy, my older brother a single man, passed away in 2011. Georgia took over his estate and managed all of his affairs with the kids. It really was a challenge for us as she held property in San Diego, California, and Lake Havasu City, Arizona. Of course, at that time we were also managing my mother, and her care in assisted living facilities in Chandler, and later in Phoenix. In 2014 Mom passed away and her affairs were dealt with again with Georgia at the helm, and we decided to sell our home in Chandler and move to Prescott, Arizona. I do not regret the move at all and we loved our time together on the mountain without little man Bugs.

We traveled the world together me and Georgia and had a grand time of it all. We were free to go and come as we wished and we did go places.

Lost her to Cancer in July 2020.

Poems Along The Way

Spud

growing up the way I did, was the best that I could do
never feeling unloved at all, having family as I grew

every day was endless wonder, my dog was there with me
we always had great adventures and exciting things to see

time went past the days stretched on, I found as I got bigger
in that time as Spud got older, he began to lose his vigor

he didn't run and jump as well, and laid a around a lot
seemed he got tired quicker, couldn't run just barely trot

came the day he wouldn't get up, he just didn't want to
within a few days he was gone, wasn't nothing I could do

on the desert, outside of town, I found a place with shade
buried Spud with honor and grace, his memory will never fade

I look back on the times we had, together in the sun
my pal, my best friend, there'll never be another one

all the years since I lost my friend, I remember times to tell
my first love in all this world, was that old dog I knew so well

Gotta Try

sitting on the fence just watching the boys
breaking in some new riding stock
hitting the ground with hurtful sound
then staggering a bit from the shock

they were having a time taking turns
trying hard to stay in the saddle
till the brute settled down to a walk
without getting their brains all a rattle

I was having fun sitting in the sun
till one of the boys said I should
climb aboard one of those nags
I'd show them some guts if I would

said I'd like to try with a gleam in my eye
so up on old dynamite I went
I tried and fought but my fate had been bought
right straight out of hell he'd been sent

round and around he'd jump I'd fall down
and over and over again
I never did learn which key I should turn
to stop that ride in the end

I've rode many broncs and been thrown many times
to this day I'd still have to say
on my first wild ride that first broke my hide
is a memory for a lifetime will stay.

Billy and the Bay

I knew a man, one hell of a man
and he had himself a dark bay horse
was a roping horse, hell of a roping horse
together they roped for money

many an event they traveled to
over many a country mile
won the money most every time
saying Shit Howdy with a great big smile

the horse was savvy to the ways of steers
knowing which way to go left or right
the roper knew just when to fire
fast catch, throw em down, tie em tight

nobody was faster with a pigging string
than this man who rode the dark bay
was the team everyone had to be beat
when the man and Duke roped that day

man was my brother, Billy by name
the stud was Duke, in his prime
roping the game for money and fame
by god he was fast with his time

years have past surely nothing lasts
Billy and Duke were gold in their day
I alone recall the thrill of it all
watching Billy rope on that Bay

My Big Brother

sun will rise on a brand new day
as we together step out of the gray
coffee in hand to stand and listen
give God thanks I hear Billy say

as it was in times long gone
I can hear his favorite song
a smile, a tear, a remembered word
one or the other lingers long

older brother so big and strong
made me define right from wrong
he cut the bonds of doubts and fears
and gave me the strength to hold on

he lives within my heart and soul
the times we lived never grow old
when all is said in the time I spend
I cherish his memories as if gold

put dirt on your hurt he would say
and I would listen and mind
the mystical, magical dirt of Yuma
to make me well every time

gone not forgotten we are together
for all this life till I reach the other
and I get to see him once again
thanks and love to my big brother

Getting Bent

was a bronc there in a stall that I didn't want to ride
they held her down they kept her still until I could decide
"throw a leg across her boy lets pay yer dues outside
else she's gonna hurt herself it's yer time now to ride"

wishes are like candy, sweet when first they're tasted
in the end, the dream you wish will get you dam near wasted
but I came here to ride this girl or know the reason why
so up aboard this dynamite package, tell mom I said goodby

open the gate and let her fly let's see what hell has got
marked her out for sure with flare and she set in to plot
first she went this way round and then she went back to that
lost my firm grip on the rein and then I lost my hat

settled down to make this ride I had a plan myself
she wasn't gonna throw me down or stuff me on a shelf
then she did her sunfish stunt and showed the world her belly
my face hit the back of her neck and my nose turned into jelly

red stuff flew across the sky and I was dumb and senseless
then she threw me in the air and I landed on top the fences
busted n' cut from head to gut I was done for in an instant
but I had made the count of eight it paid to be persistent

I'd like to thank my lucky stars for allowing me that day
to show the world a boy from Yuma could ride a bronc that way
my brother said he's never seen anything like that before
I walked out of the arena busted nose, broken ribs, high score

Bruce Holding on For the 8 Second Buzzer

Ribbon made of Stone

On the edge of the desert stands a stone border
Built in sand without water, brick, or mortar
Marvel of the landscape, the scale of all in sight
Lowly desert floor, then granite's rising might
The stone fortress rising to capture the eye
Hundreds of feet tall sheer rock to the sky
Follow the trail West, marked Interstate 8
Casa Grande, Gila Bend, Yuma's Crossing Gate
All the way down from atop Looking Glass
Up, and through man made Telegraph Pass
I'm certain the stone is to hold back the sand
Give direction to wind as it decorates the land
In sand and stone, where life is harsh and bare
Plants n' trees grow, with a father's loving care
Critters have adapted to this hot and arid space
Living in sand n' stone, within this desert place
Desert land, shifting sand, with markers to atone
Held in time immortal by a Ribbon made of Stone

Glory Bound Train

before dad left this world he said he knew Jesus
and could hear his Lord calling him home
he knew in his heart that once he'd depart
that he would never again be alone
said he had his ticket all paid up in full
to board that glory bound train
it was leaving at dawn and he said he'd be on
next stop to see family again
he looked up from bed and smiled as he said
son, do you have your ticket in hand
will it get you aboard that glory bound train
and allow me to see you again
I told him yes sir I'm going there too
but it'll take a little bit longer
I'll be there to board that glory bound train
my faith couldn't be any stronger
alright then I'll go but I'll be at the door
on the platform down at the station
where the glory bound train drops us all off
to meet and greet our relations
in this world we're alone without train fare home
no ticket, no money, no pass
to get where we're going we need to believe
with faith in our Lord that will last
I'll be going aboard that glory bound train
Dad, as soon as our Master calls me
I've got my ticket right here in my hand
my faith in my God assures me

Favorite Buckle

a buckle won in a rodeo made of silver and of gold
I did my best to win it for my Dad to have and hold

Mom said he wore the thing every time he got dressed up
most times he'd just hold it drinking coffee in his cup

never said how proud he was I had given him that prize
Mom said he held it often and it sparkled in his eyes

perhaps a part of Dad's past was in that shiny buckle
he had done the same as I and busted up a knuckle

reason I rode for that buckle is a story needs be told
so Dad could see me become a man before we both got old

he knew that it was dangerous riding for buckles and such
he was my biggest fan but he never let on too much

I moved on with my life away from my Yuma home
went back to visit often with a family of my own

years passed - the kids got older and time took its toll
Dad - then in his eighties - still had that buckle he could hold

Mom gave the buckle back to me shortly after Dad died
a note from Dad was on it and when I read it, man, I cried

"I don't have the words to say thank you near enough
You have been my inspiration whenever things got tough
Thanks for the loan, it meant a lot, sure is pretty in the sun
When it comes to winning buckles boy - You are number one
Love, Dad"
holds more meaning now than it ever did before
a buckle for my father - he never asked for more

A Gift

many a year since I started my journey
baby steps for a boy into a man
hot and cold the seasons came
in a landscape covered in sand

taking chances to get ahead
finding paths already taken
learning from mistakes I made
found the will to not be shaken

never lost the center line of life
not always on the straight and narrow
sometimes took the crooked and wide
got cut often down to the marrow

in all the bad I had to deal with
something to learn was always there
to show me why it wasn't wrong
gave a reason to grow and care

never really found the good
clean living is said to bring
then I met a little greek girl
for her finger a wedding ring

I no longer live for taking risk
try to fill in the blanks where I can
boy to adult in such a short time
learning now to live as a man

Don's Place

down off 8th Street just North of Avenue B
Don owned a place where horses were a fascination to me
six horses were boarded there I looked after five
was a Black Stud kept by himself so the others could survive
he was said to be mean which kept him alone in his stall
Don said the meanness wouldn't allow him around at all
just a boy of ten and to the Black Stud took to getting close
something no one did but I was more curious than most
seems the Black wanted a friend and I was the one he chose
he really was a gentile soul and wanted me to rub his nose
turns out he was lonely as no one would be his friend
kept people and horses at a distance acting as mean as sin
but Patch and I got to know about our secrets kept inside
I overcame my fear of him, he let go of his meanness side
over a number of weeks we spent every day together
waiting patiently for the day I'd try riding him with leather
feeling like I had to, one day I climbed up on his back
didn't have no halter, saddle, headstall, or any tack
Patch seemed to understand the simple wishes of a boy
slowly with me he walked around as gentile as a toy
riding around for weeks when no one else could see
when I tried to tell Brother Billy he just laughed at me
Don said "Just a boy making stories to add suspense"
I told them I'd show them if they'd stay behind the fence
Patch never did like Don, brother Billy he just ignored
stomping like a bull to get out they said that I'd get gored
I turned him out to be with me and he followed me all around
using the fence to climb aboard their jaws nearly hit the ground
I got to know the mean Black Stud by starting to rub his nose
we learned about each other cause that's how friendship grows
I'm just saying kindness prevails when all the bravado ends
to this day I remember Patch and how we became close friends

Birthing

Don kept as a broodmare Zona 6 years and bright
a golden palomino her mane and tail were white

carrying a foal for 6 months she was starting to show
people there had to tell me cause I sure didn't know

she loved for me to ride her guess I didn't weight a dime
always wanting my attention at anyplace and anytime

came the night to have her foal and I was there to learn
my being there not a problem as she laid down in her turn

the Vet was there to help her if any help was needed
the glory of creation with birth began as she proceeded

amazed and overcome with joy I had never beheld such wonder
I saw life start and I was struck by it, as if by rolling thunder

of all things in this big bad world that I have ever seen
birthing of a foal was like nothing that I could dream

the struggle for foal to get to his feet and find his mothers teat
I'll tell you there is nothing finer in a boy's life made to fit

I remember that very night and I guess I always will
the miracle of the birth I saw, lives within me still

Just A Sprout

mom made Lye Soap in a tub out back
dad's greasy clothes looked right off the rack
hard time living made a body learn
hold on tight to that which you earn

both folks sewed clothes using a pattern
sewing at night, with light of a lantern
western clothes that were really swell
so good in fact they had some to sell

watched every dime, traded for most need
grew a big garden with five mouths to feed
worked on the side for eggs, milk, and meat
always had enough food for all of us to eat

old house, one tub, three boys bathed in turn
homemade ice cream with a hand crank churn
Mom cooked and cleaned, wash hung out to dry
Dad an auto mechanic was a hard-working guy

evenings on front porch, radio playing inside
streetlights and bugs, watched as cars drove by
nights out on wooden beds, wet sheets on a line
posts in cans o' turpentine, no critters made it fine

Sunday to Church, head bowed when we prayed
Mom's best-fried chicken, back yard table in the shade
being a boy was better than I would ever know
family built on love still makes my heart glow

Pen

Riding My Dreams

Uncle Fergie called him Pen, said he was past his prime
working horse retired, needed help if I had the time

didn't know anything about horses, but I came to see
friendship has no age limit if both parties can agree

I was to learn to feed and water and also to clean his stall
exercise, ride, to know him, learn his ways and all

looked at me with calm and ease, had no fear of what he saw
I wasn't sure I could do the job, just a boy and I was small

slowly I learned about grooming, how to water, how to feed
slow being the main word 'cause to hurry there was no need

walked on the old dirt road, passed farm machinery and such
in time he grew to trust me and to accept my friendly touch

off the lead, away from feed, he'd follow me anywhere
he liked for me to brush him, he liked me being there

was an old riding saddle but I left it on the rack
just grab a handful of hair to climb upon his back

got along fine me and him with the time we spent together
love to be with him again in the heat of summer weather

no going back, my friend is gone and I have fully grown
memories of golden days and old Pen are deeply sown

Lost in Time

hometowns live within us, forever held spellbound
it's legends versus reality, whenever the truth is found

letting go of childhood past is more than just survival
trying to recapture memories is no reason for revival

used to go see my folks, I'm sure you will agree
traveling back to another time is how it seemed to me

the house had stayed the same with memories of the past
it's where the mold was made and a little boy was cast

always looking for the times and places that preceded
memories of that little boy in times I thought I needed

folks and house are gone now and home for me as well
the adventures of that little boy still live in me to tell

leaving that town was never very difficult for me
nothing there I wanted and nothing more to see

closed my mind but left my heart open a little bit
people an' places faded in memories that never fit

I'm no longer drawn to Yuma, nothing there to find
except a little boy who calls to me with stories lost in time

Tied in Yuma Sand

old spurs didn't fit
too wide for my heal
so I tied em on
over and under in the deal

thick leather strips
tied to boots just right
had me riding tools
snugged down hat band tight

spurs tied to my boots
felt near bulletproof
made kind of a jingle
wearing a wolfs tooth

set to do some raking
making my moves count
flying boot heal rhythm
spurring out that mount

made a heap a difference
in my style for any ride
round rowels n' smooth
safe for horses hide

I have those riding spurs
to hold here in my hand
same old leather strips
once tied in Yuma Sand

The Will to Try

didn't know the best was coming
in my youth with childhood fleeting
every trial and error drumming
learning fast and then repeating

gain was made by fear repressing
hold the line reaching skyward
spurs raking, no room for guessing
'ride for eight' the only byword

grit and grip were my essential
put dirt on it was the way
win a buckle as your credential
keep trying harder every day

couldn't know of character forming
as the times began to change
riding high as skies were storming
night and day becoming strange

with every fall comes understanding
get back up and try again
never had a comfortable landing
trying to join the ranks of men

I could see what it was I wanted
keep on trying was the only way
score high and be undaunted
character earned to this very day

looking back on the time I spent
riding leather with denim high

Riding My Dreams

getting twisted and getting bent
but never losing the will to try

what it took to win a buckle
to keep a living memory
my last straining knuckle
what rodeo means to me

Me and Gramps

Ages 3 & 4
big leather chair on a screened-in Arizona porch
pipe, tobacco, carving knife, and a Zippo pocket torch

sipping black coffee and mumbling to himself
I could sit and watch for hours I was his little elf

then as he stirred he would leave to shuffle off
then directly shuffle back and plop down with a gaff

he would tell me stories bout his growing to a man
shooting game and working, finding gold in a pan

growing up in high country, not this desert flatland here
was always game for hunting elk, bear and occasional deer

do some wood carving with his knives there on the desk
making animal figurines from the place he loved best

those were the animals he craved, the ones he knew the most
appeared to him all the time they was like living critter ghosts

and as he told his stories I would live the dreams with him
out in the forest we'd see blades of grass every tree and limb

often he'd drift off to sleep and I'd wait till he came around
sit and keep my place with him never making any sound

me and gramps we were the boys of every waking day
till one day he just wasn't there he had up and gone away

I figured he went out in the woods to hunt and hike and play
one day I too will go that way when I am old and gray

Brawley Cattle Call

a long drive to get there with my new shirt to tuck
had polished up my ropers in Billy's pickup truck

Little Britches Rodeo and had a mind to try
ride a bronc for eight and outscore the other guy

need to win a buckle to show folks I did it right
hold a piece a rope, swallow 'n' spit with fright

feet up and start to spur, beat her at the throws
watch her pull her head and stick with her as she goes

life is like a bucking chute, some never clear the gate
those that do get to ride hanging on to make the eight

hitting the ground for sure makes you rethink your game
get back up and try again or you will never be the same

rodeo ain't for everyone, at one time it was for me
lots o' times I got thrown, no time, no points you see

Billy said with every hurt put dirt on it and try again
my brother helped me understand what it took to be a man

it's all about the way you find the courage and the pride
face your fear, hang on tight, to make an eight-second ride

For a Buckle

lost my boot in the chute
lost my stirrup as well
took a good shot to the chin
damn near rang my bell

not the way I wanted to go
but I gave it all till the end
finished high in the standings
eight stitches to close my chin

then went home to Momma
had to own up to the game
learned about keeping secrets
not telling's a lie just the same

here's the buckle I won at the fair
Billy said I showed 'em real grit
Momma was hurt that I hid the truth
like being honest didn't matter a bit

didn't want to lie to Momma
not telling about rodeo that way
I cried to know she was hurt
still carry that guilt to this day

being a boy in a man's world
brings changes we can never see
deep are scars on chins and hearts
that buckle still means that to me

Number On His Shirt

both of us came from Yuma right on the Arizona line
Billy came to do some tripping I came to ride for time

folks there knew Billy and Duke had seen them many a time
but nothing about his little brother a kid standing there in line

"Pleased to have you try your luck" said the man taking my fee
"We'll get started directly got several riders" other than me

"I came to win a buckle if you're given them away"
said "You'll have to stay aboard till the count an eight"

said "I'm over from Yuma way" He said "That's mighty swell"
pinning a number on my shirt so's the judges there could tell

over drinking coffee was Billy with Duke in a holding stall
ropers always go first and they were waiting for the call

won't bore you with details about the day's events and score
I got hurt, we both won buckles, that we've never wore

driving the road back to Yuma, we were joking and having fun
Billy was really happy said Duke never had a better run

just a kid growing up and getting hurt on horses in the dirt
loving life and making memories with a number on his shirt

Corner in Time

three fifteen Tuesday afternoon
the wind was blowing a bit
raking hay for old man Ramsey
so dry I couldn't hardly spit

stopped at P's on Old 95
only place with anything cold
got to get me an RC Cola
gum and a pack a Old Gold

little old place where beer and sodas
are kept outside in a box
just right of the front screen door
where the lid is held down with a rock

had himself just one old pump
sold him some gas time to time
mostly it's beer, cold soda pop,
smokes, and a pint if you're buy'n

place used to be a real busy stop
for farmers and laborers and such
business is gone, the road got improved
people don't stop there as much

Pete's Corner for a number of years
but now it's just P's Store
gas pump is gone, a sign of the times
nobody buys his gas anymore

but on any hot day in the valley
a cold drink will fit you just right

Riding My Dreams

keep you from fading away in the heat
waiting for the cool of the night

soon P's will close and go by the way
you can't stop time or bad luck
I'll miss P's where the beer was cold
and the sodas were two for a buck

everything's fine at P's corner in time
screen door will never have a lock
sodas and beer in the box out front
where the lid is held down with a rock

One-Eyed Jacks

I was young when my father told me
about people he dealt with and knew
they show you only one side of themselves
the other side is kept from view

without seeing both sides of people
you will never know what they will do
cheat the deal in the card game of life
which meant they would cheat on you

my father had a name for these people
and I learned as I started to grow
he called them all one-eyed jacks
was no better way for me to know

some have their best side showing
the other side they don't reveal
doesn't mean they will cheat you
pay attention to see if they're real

met many people and kept it in mind
to watch for the face they don't show
if they only show as a one-eyed jack
then pass them by and let them go

never have been disappointed
when I look for the other side
of the people I know and deal with
all one-eyed jacks till they're tried

Late December

boy on leave from the Navy
girl still going to high school
searching for love and affection
both of them acting the fool

thinking this could be forever
not knowing what love means
a boy n' a girl in dad's old truck
two kids still in their teens

of all the things I remember
what came first was best
young girl with a lonely sailor
winters night getting undressed

coming of age in that little town
couldn't happen at a better time
a boy and a girl in a hurry
to cross that forbidden line

time passed quickly for the boy
forgot about the girl still waiting
didn't care much for her affection
left her home anticipating

foggy memories of by-gone days
but I can still remember
growing up fast in that pickup truck
on a winters night in late December

Brand New Pair of Boots

second hand boots sure didn't fit me well
tight in places and caused my feet to swell

all I had to try my luck at riding
hurt so bad I had to look to buying

San Luis Old Mexico, Frito said he could
make a pair a boots, to fit just like they should

doscientos, but said he'd make them for eighty
custom fit, one weeks time to have them ready

for custom made you have to pay first
waiting a week I thought my head would burst

but I paid upfront for some brand-new scoots
uno semana he said I'd have my custom boots

red n blue cabro piel made my face grin
neuvas botas, Gracias Tacones, my friend

well made and perfect fit what a total joy
hermosas botas siempre quiera for this boy

60 years since then a way back in my roots
never will forget my brand new pair of boots

Zona

She was a beauty - to me anyway
I took to liking her that very first day
We kinda bonded as I learned her name
Like a 8x10 photo in a 8x10 frame

Went often to see her she was a sight
Hair like gold in the bright morning light
Stately and Proud in every way
Remembering back 60 years I would say

Such a lady that I came to know
As a boy with her she watched me grow
Learning about her took all my time
Playing it over again in my mind

Everything for me was new with her
Doing the things I hoped she'd prefer
Bagged for delivery and due any time
12 months pregnant and she was prime

Her name was Zona she was 8 years old
I watched her give birth to her fourth foal
Amazing to watch God's hand at play
To see new life emerge that way

Horses are unique and sent from God
Special lives to live and roads to be trod
Love and understanding that they have for us
Is built on mutual respect and trust

Early On

running over some early footage of memories in my mind
looking for happy days amongst the vintage of that time

times were bright, and I was light on my feet a way back then
a boy with dreams of bigger things than stick horses and a grin

seemed my days though all the haze were focused on watching men
I wanted to be what I could see and to grow up fast back then

this wild-eyed boy found horses, and to Rodeo Sport I was treated
doing my best to pass the test and become the man I sorely needed

Billy told me to get better required me to work on winning
something above the thoughts of a boy I had in the beginning

putting together a winning plan, meant something besides the fun
being successful riding horses, was a dream come true in the Sun

in those days, living cowboy ways, I found my life was turning
I wanted more than I had at home, or the ways that I was learning

I turned eighteen on Christmas Day the year was Sixty Four
the following month I left that town on a US Navy tour

when I came back after military life my world had really changed
didn't care about boots and spurs my goals were rearranged

I moved on with the rest of my life, no horses to be a part
but they remain deep in my soul, and always in my heart

'Bout 10 Miles From Home

back many years, on leave from Navy
Somerton, Az. asphalt heat was wavy

another Annual Tamale Festival
eat great food and be restful

was a Rodeo to my surprise
best ride wins a buckle prize

folks were Mexican and Cocopah mix
tamales, broncs, a buckle just for kicks

was a girl I knew sitting in the stands
I had nothing but time on my hands

she said she knew me from years before
didn't know her name, memory was poor

"could I take you to a drive inn picture show?"
"I don't date cowboys" she turned away to go

shot down for sure, nothing more was said
her skin-tight wranglers dancing in my head

looking back she'd make this one exception
was on my way to finding loves redemption

Somerton, Tamales, a buckle of chrome
horses, and a girl, bout 10 miles from home

Just After the Rain

one mile up does Prescott lie
where hills n' dells meet the sky

rain comes to clean the town

fog recedes with vision plain
all is clear just after the rain

wondrous sight when rain does fall

air is crisp having been washed clean
better to breathe than it's ever been

peace in all its glorious refrain
could it be heaven just after the rain

if ever was an Eden on earth
if ever was a place of worth

if my dreams could take me there
if my eyes could vision share

I want to live out all my days
in my Prescott just after the rain

Epilogue

Little Britches Rodeo events were the starting point for a young boy growing up in Southwest Arizona. Yuma was the town where I was born and raised. Heat and Bright Sunlight are the staple weather in Yuma. Sitting in the Sonoran Desert at 200 feet elevation the mainstay of business is Military and Farming. Being only 24 miles from the Mexican Border a very strong Mexican influence is prevalent in that community. Horses, horse property, and horse people were common in that rural place. It seemed logical that I would take an interest in horses at a young age. My brother Billy was very connected to the sport of timed steer roping and was a natural lead into my introduction to bronc riding. I never did contemplate a career in the rodeo world, or of turning professional with my riding. As I turned 18 years old and Little Britches Rodeo events came to a close I turned my attention to leaving that small town. The way I chose to leave was with the US Navy and wanting to learn a trade to follow. Walking away from horses was not easy for me spiritually or mentally but I had to do it to get on with whatever was in store for me down the road. Once having left that part of my life I never looked back, nor set in a saddle again, except as a Motorcycle Policeman for the majority of my eight years with the City of Tempe, Arizona Police Department. I always considered that Harley Davidson I rode to be an Iron Horse, and the seat of that machine a saddle.

My next career was as a delivery driver for United Parcel Service. Did that for 12 years and then went into management for the next 18 years. Started with United Parcel Service in 1977 and ended that work in 2007, for a total of 30 years. I always told myself to finish what you start. I quit being a policeman in 1977 and stopped going to college that same year. My new job did not lend itself to attending college due to the long working hours as a UPS man. After retiring in 2007 I did go back to ASU and finished my degree work for a college degree in Criminal Justice. Showed it to my mother and she was very proud of me for keeping my promise to get that piece of paper. I have often thought about going back to college for more learning and another degree, but don't want to start something I may not have the time on this earth to finish. Don't start it unless you plan to finish it. I wish marriage carried that same drive to continue, but when two people are making decisions in a venture it never runs smooth, or so it seemed for me.

Billy passed away in 2011, my mother passed in 2014, and that same year I moved with my wife Georgia, to Prescott, Arizona, and here I plan to stay.

Lost my wife Georgia, in 2020 and have worked on getting better at dealing with the loss, which I believe I have accomplished for the most part. Learning early on in my life about getting knocked down and getting back up to keep going has helped me and shown me the way to keep doing just that. They say learning has not occurred until behavior changes. Over the years of my life, I have had to change my behavior often, so I would guess a lot of learning has occurred in that time. They also tell us we never stop learning. I'm of the opinion I still have a lot of learning to get done before I check out of this life.

Now at age 76, the pace of life has slowed. Widowed and living in Prescott, Arizona gives me time to reflect on the years and the life I have lived.

I am so glad to live on this mountain and away from the desert heat, the noise, the traffic, and the crime, of the Phoenix Valley. I have a good deal of physical aches and pains associated with my early activities with horses, but I feel it was worth every bit of it for the fact that I did what I wanted to do. I wanted to be accepted into the man's world as I saw it and bronc riding was the way for me. Billy, my older brother, was my guide and my mentor in the time I spent with horses, I could not have done it without him.

In the past few months, I even took the time to reconnect with a woman I wrote about in my adventures. She was my heart throb in high school that I never talked to or got to know. It was not a good meeting but gave me the chance to close the circle on that factor in my life. Finished the relationship and made the dream a reality which I could put behind me and move on. It is incredible that I carried that dream for some 60-plus years and was able to make it go away, as they say in a court of law, with prejudice. Most people don't get that opportunity, or when they do, don't take the time to deal with it. She was not the girl I wanted her to be and she never was. Wishing for something you don't need can come true, and when it does you often don't want it. Among the many things I carry with me are the joys of winning and the downside of losing. Some I tell, and some I keep hidden away in that personal space that is for me and me alone. From boy, to man, to old man, life still has wonder and meaning. I know the two most important days of my life. The day I was born, and the day I found out why. The day

I realized why I was born was the day I met my wife Georgia. In the twelve years we were married I found out how to live. I truly found the joy in my life with her and yes, I shared it with others. Every one of us can do that as well. Been a hell of a ride all in all.

Ω

Author's Bio

Bruce D. Sparks was born and raised in Yuma, Arizona. He resided in the East Valley of Phoenix for many years and currently lives in Prescott, Arizona. His Military service was followed by Law Enforcement, then United Parcel Service for 30 years, and finally retirement. Recalling the vivid details and memories of the exciting times of his life as a boy in Yuma and elsewhere, Bruce put pen to paper and began writing stories and reflections of his early years. As he reflected on the writings of his early years, he continued the saga and continued writing about his life and his memories. Simple things such as Hunting, Camping, Fishing, and everything outdoors were his life in Arizona as he knew it. Now it's life in Prescott and time to remember, reflect, and to continue his passion for writing.

Riding My Dreams

Riding My Dreams

Made in the USA
Las Vegas, NV
16 June 2023